2 HOUR CRAFTING Treasures

Edited by Laura Scott

HOUSE of
WHITE
BIRCHES

PUBLISHERS
SINCE 1947

Editor: Laura Scott
Technical Editor: Läna Schurb
Associate Editor: June Sprunger
Copy Editor: Mary Nowak

Photography: Tammy Christian, Jeff Chilcote, Jennifer Fourman
Photography Assistants: Linda Quinlan, Arlou Witwer

Production Coordinator: Brenda Gallmeyer
Book Design: Shaun Venish
Book Production: Dan Kraner
Traffic Coordinator: Sandra Beres
Graphs/Drawings: Leslie Brandt, Julie Catey, Jessica Rothe, Allison Rothe

Publishers: Carl H. Muselman, Arthur K. Muselman
Chief Executive Officer: John Robinson
Marketing Director: Scott Moss
Product Development Director: Vivian Rothe
Publishing Services Manager: Brenda Wendling

Printed in the United States of America
First Printing: 1999
Library of Congress Number: 99-73197
ISBN: 1-882138-49-X

Every effort has been made to ensure the accuracy and completeness of the instructions in this book. However, we cannot be responsible for human error or for the results when using materials other than those specified in the instructions, or for variations in individual work.

Dear Crafter,

Are you a busy person? If you're nodding your head, or even chuckling over this somewhat ridiculous question (after all, who isn't busy these days?), then get ready to paint, stitch, glue, cut and stamp your way through this collection of more than 125 super easy and super-quick-to-craft projects! You'll remember just how much you love crafting when you actually finish a project in two hours or less! You'll be delighted to actually finish all the projects you start!

And, as our title says, these projects aren't tacky little gadgets that will just collect dust on your shelves. These projetcts are treasures—cute, fun, colorful and unique treasures—bound to win the attention of all who see them. Whether you make your crafts to sell at craft shows, or as gifts throughout the year for family and friends, you're sure to have a ball crafting and sharing these projects.

If you're one of those crafters who likes to dabble in just about every medium, you'll be tickled pink with the variety of techniques and applications in this collection. From painting to woodcrafts to fimo clay sculpting to paper crafts to no-sew appliqué and much more, beginning crafters as well as more advanced crafters will enjoy expanding their skills while creating these unique projects.

Maybe I'm just partial because I've worked on this book from start to finish, but I really believe this book has something for every crafter. We've included charming country crafts, easy wearable crafts, simple crafts for kids to do, money-making bazaar crafts, and holiday crafts galore! With the simple and complete instructions and clear templates and diagrams, we've taken the guesswork out of crafting so you'll spend more time with your creative hobby and less time guessing what to do next.

I hope you have as much fun crafting the projects in this book as my staff and I had in bringing them to you in this volume.

Warm regards,

Laura Scott

Editor
2-Hour Crafting Treasures

Contents

Wearable Crafts

Country Crafts

Last-Minute Gifts

Bazaar Bestsellers

The Night Before Christmas

Just for Kids

Every Day's a Holiday

Country Crafts

Bird
Seed
Grow
Your
Own
Birds

Whether you make country crafts to sell at craft shows, to give as special gifts, or simply to add warm and friendly touches to your home, you're sure to enjoy crafting this collection of charming projects!

"Grow Your Own Birds"

No wonder these bluebirds are happy — they've taken up residence in the bird seed bucket! Your bird-feeding friends will chuckle again and again over this whimsical design. It's a snap to paint!

Design by Delores F. Ruzicka

Materials

- 4" x 6" piece Rust It thin tin from Tolin' Station
- Tin snips
- Awl or hammer and nail
- Stovepipe wire
- Ceramcoat acrylic paints from Delta Technical Coatings Inc.:
  Blue jay #2059
  Georgia clay #2097
  Blue mist #2400
  Light ivory #2401
  Black #2506
  Blueberry #2513
- American Painter paintbrushes from Loew-Cornell:
  Series #4300 sizes 6 and 4
  Series #4000 size 1
- Stencil for ¼" checks
- Pencil

Project Notes

Let paint dry before applying overlaying or adjacent colors.

Refer to photo throughout.

Instructions

1. Referring to pattern, cut shape from tin. Punch hole in each upper corner for hanging using awl or hammer and nail.

2. Paint birds with blue mist, shading them lightly with blue jay. Paint beaks with Georgia clay. Paint eyes with black; add a tiny dot of light ivory to highlight each eye.

3. Using #6 brush, paint label with light ivory; highlight with blue mist and blueberry. When dry, add "Bird Seed" lettering with black paint and #1 brush.

4. Using #1 brush and light ivory, paint "Grow Your Own Birds" on unpainted portion of tin.

5. Using stencil, paint bottom in checkerboard pattern alternating light ivory and blueberry.

6. For hanger, coil stovepipe wire around pencil; pull wire ends to stretch out coils. Attach wire ends through holes in sign. ❁

"No Henpeckin' Allowed"

If a country home is indeed a happy home, perhaps it is because of "house rules" like this one! You'll enjoy making and giving this gift using precut wooden shapes and simple painting and sewing techniques.

Design by Rochelle Norris

Materials

- 5" x 2½" x 2½" straw bale
- Wooden products from Woodworks:
  2½" apple #FF-AP10
  5¼" picket fence #ST-F525
  3 chickens #CO-4525
  Milk can #TC-20MC
  3½" ribbon #CO-9924
  2 eggs #FF-E075
  Milk bottle #LB-MILK
  1 pair mitten hands #CO-9327
- Bamboo skewers: 4" and 2 (6")
- 10" ¼"-diameter wooden dowel
- Americana acrylic paints from DecoArt:
  Titanium (snow) white #DA1
  Buttermilk #DA3
  Burnt umber #DA64
  Lamp (ebony) black #DA67
  Cool neutral #DA89
  Warm neutral #DA90
  Raw sienna #DA93
  Mississippi mud #DA94
  Rookwood red #DA97
  Honey brown #DA163
  Light buttermilk #DA164
  Driftwood #DA171

- Golden Taklon paintbrushes from Loew-Cornell:
  #2–#12 shader or flat brushes
  ¾" wash brush
  10/0 liner brush
- Waxed paper
- Double-ended stylus
- Rose cosmetic blusher
- Cotton swab
- Pens from Sakura of America:
  .02, .03 and .05 black Pigma pens
  Identi Pen black marking pen
- 8" x 10" white poster board
- Torn 12" x 17" print fabric rectangle for shirt
- Torn 1" x 24" strip coordinating fabric
- 5" straw hat
- Matching heavy-duty threads and hand-sewing needle
- Polyester fiberfill
- Natural raffia
- Medium- and heavy-weight jute twine
- Dried Spanish moss
- 2 (9") pieces 20-gauge wire
- Drill with ⅟₁₆", ³⁄₃₂" and ¼" bits
- 2 small eye screws
- Hot-glue gun and glue sticks
- Pencil

Project Notes

Refer to Project Notes for "Special Mum" on page 35.

Head & Hands

1. Refer to Head & Hands instructions for "Special Mum," page 35, substituting wooden apple for ball, and base-coating head and hands with warm neutral; highlight with buttermilk and shade with Mississippi mud.

2. Referring to Fig. 1, finish hands and face as for "Special Mum" except instead of stippling cheeks, add a few freckles to blushed cheeks with fine-line marking pen.

Additional Painting & Finishing

1. *Fence:* Base-coat with driftwood; highlight with cool neutral and shade with Mississippi mud. Speckle fence lightly with black. Using .05 Pigma pen, lightly sketch outlines on pickets and crosspieces.

2. *Milk can:* Base-coat with driftwood; highlight with cool neutral and shade with Mississippi mud. Using Identi Pen, write "Farm Fresh" on milk can with fine tip; add dots to ends of lines in letters with broad tip.

3. *Chickens:* Referring to Fig. 2, paint two chickens facing

Fig. 1

Fig. 2

right and one facing left. Base-coat chickens with raw sienna; highlight with honey brown and shade with burnt umber. Lightly speckle chickens with black. Dot on eyes with small stylus point dipped in black. Stipple tail feathers, combs and wattles with rookwood red. Define wings with elongated comma strokes of burnt umber; paint beaks honey brown.

4. *Milk bottle:* Base-coat with light buttermilk; highlight with titanium white and shade with cool neutral. With fine tip of Identi Pen, write "Milk" on bottle; add dots to ends of lines with broad tip.

5. *Eggs:* Base-coat with light buttermilk; highlight with titanium white and shade with cool neutral. Speckle eggs lightly with burnt umber.

6. *Sign:* Base-coat wooden ribbon with light buttermilk; highlight with titanium white and shade with buttermilk. Speckle lightly with burnt umber. Using Pigma pen, outline sign; add lettering, "No henpeckin' allowed," and dots with Identi Pen.

Clothing

1. Referring to instructions for "Special Mum," follow steps 1–7 in instructions for "Clothing." Use patterns for poster-board shirt and fabric shirt on pages 157 and 158.

2. Cut 24" fabric strip in half for shoulder straps; tie knot in each end. Glue one knot of each to front of shirt and drape straps over shoulders; cross straps in back and glue knots in place.

3. Wrap several strands of raffia around neck; tie in bow in front.

Hair & Hat

1. Cut 6" lengths of medium- and heavy-weight jute. Fold each piece in half; glue to top of head.

2. Glue hat in place; trim hair to desired length.

Assembly

1. *Sign with eggs:* drill small hole in each end of sign and though top of each egg. Coil one end of each piece of wire around a pencil. Thread straight end of one piece through sign from front to back; thread on one egg. Repeat with remaining wire and egg on other side of sign. Thread straight ends of wire through holes in hands and twist to hold sign and eggs securely in place.

2. Apply glue to end of wooden dowel and stick into center top of straw bale.

3. Glue fence to front of straw bale. Glue left-facing chicken to base of fence at right.

4. Glue small clump of Spanish moss to top of hat

where chicken will "nest"; glue chicken to hat atop moss. Glue 4" skewer to back of third chicken; apply glue to other end and insert in straw bale on left side in front.

5. Insert eye screws into tops of milk bottle and milk can. String bottle and can on single strand of jute; knot in a loop and hang from fence. ●

Country Angel Ornaments

Imagine these little charmers adorning your country tree, or decorating your gift packages, or stitched together in a wonderful swag to drape across your mantel. The possibilities are endless!

Design by Chris Malone

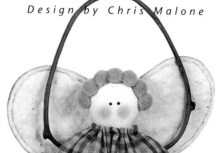

Materials

Each Ornament

- 3½" x 5½" piece natural muslin
- 4½" x 10" piece homespun plaid fabric
- 3" x 6" piece natural cotton batting
- 3" x 6" brown kraft paper
- Polyester fiberfill
- Toothpick
- Brown acrylic paint
- Cosmetic blusher
- Cotton-tip swab
- Craft glue
- 7 (¼") tan pompoms
- 1½"-diameter artificial green wreath
- 6" piece ¼"-wide tan grosgrain ribbon
- 12" piece grapevine
- Sewing machine
- Hand-sewing needle
- Coordinating sewing threads
- Florist wire

Instructions

1. Fold muslin and plaid fabrics in half, right sides facing. Referring to patterns (page 151), trace one head onto doubled muslin, and one dress onto doubled plaid fabric, right side of fabric facing.

2. Assemble head by stitching along traced lines through both layers of muslin, leaving bottom (straight) edge open. Cut out, cutting ⅛" from seam; clip curves and turn head right side out. Stuff firmly with fiberfill; hand-stitch opening closed.

3. Assemble dress by stitching along traced lines through both layers of plaid fabric, leaving top (straight) edge open. Cut out, cutting ¼" from seam; clip curves and turn right side out. Fold top edge under ¼"; with sewing needle and matching thread, make a gathering stitch close to fold, beginning and ending at center back.

4. Lightly stuff dress with fiberfill; insert head and pull gathers to fit snugly around neck. Take a few stitches through neck before knotting and clipping thread.

5. Using toothpick, dot two small eyes of brown paint onto face. Using cotton swab, apply cheeks of cosmetic blusher.

6. Glue one pompom over seam at center top of head; glue three pompoms close together over seam on each side of center pompom.

7. Glue or sew wreath to front of dress. Tie ribbon in bow; trim ends. Glue bow to top of wreath.

8. Bend 12" piece of grapevine into a circle; overlap ends and secure with florist wire. Glue ends to back of angel ½" below neck.

9. Referring to pattern (page 151), trace wings onto kraft paper. Lay paper, traced side up, on wrong side of cotton batting; pin together outside traced line. Using tan thread, machine-stitch along stitched line through both thicknesses; cut out ⅛" from seam. Machine-stitch down center of wings. Glue fleece side to back of angel along stitched line. ●

Yo-Yo Basket

Yo-yos are all the rage! A favorite method for making decorative vests and wearables, the gathered fabric circles here are joined to make a distinctive home dec accent!

Design by Janice McKee

Materials

- ½ yard red print fabric
- ½ yard navy blue print fabric
- ½ yard white print fabric
- Fabric stiffener
- Plastic wrap
- Bowl to use as a mold
- Sewing Needle and thread

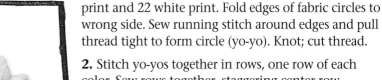

Project Note

Sample was made using a glass bowl 10¼" in diameter at the top and 6½" in diameter at the bottom for the mold. Depending on the bowl used, fewer or more yo-yos may be needed.

Instructions

1. Cut fabric into 3¼" circles: 22 red print, 22 navy print and 22 white print. Fold edges of fabric circles to wrong side. Sew running stitch around edges and pull thread tight to form circle (yo-yo). Knot; cut thread.

2. Stitch yo-yos together in rows, one row of each color. Sew rows together, staggering center row between top and bottom rows. Sew constructed piece together at side to cover sides of bowl (try on for fit), easing and sewing tighter as necessary.

3. Cut one red print 7½" circle and one navy print 7½" circle. Turn raw edges under ¼"; press. Slipstitch circles together, wrong sides facing.

4. Turn bowl upside down on work surface. Center stitched large circles (bottom of basket) on bowl bottom. Slip yo-yos (basket sides) over bowl. Pin bottom and sides together and stitch, easing in where necessary.

5. Cover bowl mold with plastic wrap. Place fabric over plastic. Following manufacturer's instructions, saturate fabric with stiffener, molding base to bowl. Let dry. ✻

Friendship Gift Box

Add a special dimension to your gift by presenting it in this colorful container. It starts off as a plain old papier-mâché box, but you transform it into a lasting reminder of your thoughtfulness and friendship.

Design by Rochelle Norris

Materials

- 9½"-diameter round papier-mâché box with lid
- Ceramcoat acrylic paints from Delta Technical Coatings Inc.:
  Maroon #2075
  Candy bar brown #2407
  Trail tan #2435
  Black #2506
  Butter cream #2523
- Paintbrush
- Spattering brush
- 6 or 7 pages from Potting Shed note pad by Main Street Press
- Vinyl-to-vinyl wallpaper paste
- Pens from Sakura of America:
  .03 Pigma black marking pen
  Identi Pen black marking pen
- Damp cloth

Project Notes

Let paint dry before applying overlaying or adjacent colors.

Refer to photo throughout.

Instructions

1. Paint lid top and box with butter cream paint. Shade outside edge of lid top with trail tan. Paint rim maroon; shade along bottom edge with candy bar brown.

2. Speckle entire box lightly with black paint.

3. Cut motifs from note paper and plan positions around sides of box. Spread wallpaper paste on back of paper motifs and position on box, wiping gently with a damp cloth to smooth out paper and remove any excess paste.

4. Cut motifs from note paper for lid; position in center as desired. Apply with wallpaper paste. Set box aside to dry for several hours.

5. Using black marking pen, write "friends are flowers in life's garden…." around top edge of box lid three times. Add dots on ends of lines in letters.

6. In blank area of each segment on side of box, write one of the following sayings, adding dots to ends of letters as shown: "from one small seed of kindness friendship grows"; "Always my sister, forever my friend"; "friends"; "If friends were flowers I'd pick you!"; or "Gardening friends really know how to hoe down." ●

Bee and Hive Plant Pokes

Dress up flower beds or pots with these whimsical pots featuring an oversized bee and jute-wrapped hive.

Designs by Donna J. Vaites

Materials

Each Project

- 18" ¼"-diameter wooden dowel
- 6" plastic foam egg
- Low-temperature glue gun and glue sticks
- Natural raffia

Bee

- White craft foam sheet
- 3½" plastic foam egg
- DecoArt patio paint:
  Sunshine yellow #DCP6
  Wrought iron black #DCP21
- Paintbrush
- 2 (¾") black pompoms
- 2 (4") pieces black chenille stem
- 2 wooden toothpicks
- Scribbles dimensional paint from Duncan Enterprises: black and yellow
- Craft stick

Hive

- 12½ yards 5-ply jute twine
- 4 small silk violets, or any small flower on a wire stem
- Several small silk ivy leaves
- Small resin bee
- Black acrylic craft paint
- Paintbrush

Project Notes

Refer to photo throughout for placement.

Bee

1. Paint smaller egg and 1¾" circle at pointed end of larger egg with black patio paint. Paint remainder of larger egg with sunshine yellow patio paint; let dry.

2. Referring to pattern (page 152), cut 2 wings from white craft foam.

3. Glue a black pompom to end of each chenille piece.

4. Insert toothpicks halfway into wide end of yellow

Continued on page 152

Pink Piggy Bank

Saving is a pleasure when you're chucking your spare change into this cutie.
He's easy to make from a leftover potato-chip canister.

Design by Helen L. Rafson

Materials

- 1.8-ounce potato-chip canister with lid
- Baby pink #053 Rainbow Felt Classic from Kunin Felt
- Ceramcoat acrylic paints from Delta Technical Coatings Inc.:
  Lisa pink #2084
  White #2505
  Black #2506
- Pink craft foam sheet
- Aleene's Thick Tacky Glue by Duncan Enterprises
- Aleene's Primer by Duncan Enterprises
- Paintbrush
- 2 (15mm) round wiggly eyes
- Black fine-tip permanent marking pen
- CMC spray-on Satin Clear Finish #07202 from Delta Technical Coatings Inc.
- Seam sealant
- 11¼" piece ⅝"-wide pink gingham ribbon from Wrights

Project Note

Refer to photo throughout.

Instructions

1. Trace around canister lid onto felt; cut out circle. Cut a 1¾" x ¼" slot in center of circle; cut matching slot in center of lid. Glue felt to top of lid. From felt, cut ¾"-wide strip long enough to go around lid edge; glue to edge of lid, matching ends neatly in back. Set aside to dry.

2. Clean and dry potato-chip canister. Coat outside with one coat of primer; let dry.

3. Paint outside of canister with three coats Lisa pink, letting paint dry between coats.

4. Dip end of paintbrush handle into white paint; dot clusters of three dots randomly over surface of painted can, redipping only after three dots are completed. Add single accent dots as desired; let dry.

5. Spray painted canister with spray-on finish; let dry.

6. Referring to pattern (below), cut one right ear from pink craft foam; reverse pattern and cut one left ear. Cut 1⅛" circle from craft foam for snout.

7. Using marking pen, draw dashed lines around canister, one ⅛" below metal rim, and another just above bottom rim. Draw dashed line around edge of snout, and around both ears on both sides.

8. Dip paintbrush handle into black paint and dot two nostrils onto pink foam snout; let dry.

9. Bend over tips of ears and glue; let dry. Glue ears, eyes and snout to can as shown.

10. Tie ribbon in bow; trim ends and coat with seam sealant. Glue bow at center bottom of canister. ❁

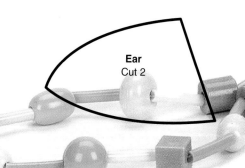

Ear
Cut 2

Perky Piglet Yo-Yo Magnet

Imagine a herd of these fine swine cavorting across the front of your fridge! You can make a whole basketful in just an evening while you catch up with your favorite television shows!

Design by Helen L. Rafson

Materials

- Pink print fabric: 3" and 5" circles
- Coordinating sewing thread and needle
- Polyester fiberfill
- 3¼" piece white pipe cleaner
- 7" piece ¼"-wide white satin ribbon
- Seam sealant
- Pink felt scraps
- ½" pink two-hole button
- 1" x ½" piece adhesive-back magnet
- Black acrylic paint
- Paintbrush
- Tacky craft glue
- Pencil

Project Note

Refer to photo throughout.

Instructions

1. Make a yo-yo from 5" fabric circle: Fold fabric edge under ¼". Sew running stitch around edge; do not knot or cut thread. Place small amount of fiberfill in center of fabric circle (do not overstuff). Pull thread tightly to form circle and enclose fiberfill; tie off and stitch opening closed. Repeat with 3" fabric circle.

2. Referring to patterns cut two triangular ears and two feet from pink felt. Glue ears to back of smaller yo-yo; let dry. Glue smaller yo-yo atop larger yo-yo.

3. Dip end of paintbrush handle into black paint; dot on eyes. Let dry. Glue on button for nose. Glue feet to back of larger yo-yo at bottom of pig; let dry.

4. Coil pipe cleaner around pencil; slide off and glue one end to back of larger yo-yo for tail; apply seam sealant to tip of tail; let dry.

5. Tie ribbon in bow; trim ends at an angle and treat ends with seam sealant; let dry. Glue bow below pig's chin. Peel adhesive from magnet; press magnet onto back of pig. ●

"Let It Snow!" Wall Hanging

After the holiday decorations come down, walls and doors can seem depressingly bare. Liven up your personal landscape with this wintry decoration! Precut tin shapes make it a snap to complete.

Design by Doxie Keller for DecoArt

Materials

- Rusty Tin-Tiques from D&CC:
  3½" x 7½" sign
  4½" x 2½" tree
  2 (4¾") snowmen
- Multipurpose sealer #DS17 from DecoArt
- Americana acrylic paints from DecoArt:
  White wash #DA2
  Ebony black #DA67
  Primary red #DA199
  Primary blue #DA200
  Primary yellow #DA201
- Loew-Cornell paintbrushes:
  Series Fab #6 round
  Series 7350 #2 liner
  Series 7300 #12 flat
- Hammer and nail
- Small piece of thin, flat wood
- Craft cement
- 24" piece 18-gauge black wire
- Needle-nose pliers
- Scraps of red plaid or pin-dot fabric
- Pencil

Project Notes

Unless instructed otherwise, let paints dry before applying adjacent or overlapping colors. Refer to photo throughout.

Instructions

1. Wipe off tin pieces and base-coat both sides with multipurpose sealer. Let dry.

2. *Tree:* Mix green paint by combining primary yellow and primary blue. Using #6 round stiff fabric brush, dab or stipple green paint on tree, working from edges toward center and leaving center unpainted.

3. *Snowmen:* Mix white wash with a tiny bit of primary blue. Using #6 round stiff fabric brush, dab or stipple paint on round sections of snowmen, working from edges toward center and leaving centers unpainted.

4. *Snowman #1:* Using #12 flat brush, paint hat ebony black. Paint hatband with green; while paint is still wet, blend in a little yellow on left side. Paint vest with green, blending in a little additional yellow to right of center seam and along bottom of right side. Using #2 liner, paint buttons primary red. Mix primary red and primary yellow to make orange; paint nose. Paint heart-shaped cheeks primary red. Outline base of nose, base of right cheek and draw mouth with ebony black.

5. *Snowman #2:* Paint hat as for Snowman #1. Do not paint a vest, but add primary red round buttons down front, blending in a little white wash while paint is still wet. Add primary red heart to left of top button. Add orange nose, black eyes and mouth; highlight eyes with white wash. Using white wash, paint two-section snow child on bottom left of snowman; stipple in just a very little light blue along outer edge while paint is wet. Add green buttons, highlighting them with yellow on left and bottom edges, and red cheeks, and dot on black eyes. Using liner brush, give snow child a hat by painting an arc of primary yellow over top of head, and then an arc of light blue (white wash mixed with primary blue) atop yellow. Using ebony black and liner brush, outline head, adding a few wispy curls; outline neckline and buttons, and define right edge of body.

6. *Sign:* Write letters with red (leave room on left side of sign for mounting tree); stripe with green. Outline letters first with white wash, then shade outlining with ebony black. Apply "drifts" of white wash atop each letter.

7. Using white wash and #6 round stiff fabric brush, spatter all pieces.

8. Using hammer and nail, punch two holes for hanger in top corners of sign; punch a hole in top of each snowman, and two holes for hanging snowmen on bottom edge of sign.

9. Cement small piece of wood to back of tree to serve as spacer; cement tree top to left side of sign. Coil wire around pencil; stretch out coils as desired. Using needle-nose pliers as needed, attach coiled wire hanger to top of sign, and hang snowmen from bottom of sign. Tear fabric into strips; tie one around each snowman's neck, and a third around hanger at top left of sign. ✻

Painted Wallpaper Pocket

This little pretty is fun to paint! It makes a lovely little decoration in an unexpected spot, and is perfectly sized to tuck into a valentine.

Design by Louy Danube

Materials

- Transfer paper
- ¼" hole punch
- White nylon net (optional)
- 13" (¼") gold cording
- Scraps of vinyl wallpaper, preferably with a linenlike texture
- Scalloped craft shears
- Sewing machine and thread
- Raspberry spray paint
- Ceramcoat acrylic paints from Delta Technical Coatings Inc.:
  Berry red #2056
  Wedgwood green #2070
  Maroon #2075
  Hunter green #2471
  Phthalo blue #2502
  White #2505
  Metallic gold #2600
- Aerosol sealer or antique finish (optional)
- Round #3 paintbrush

Instructions

1. Lay two 6" squares wallpaper together, right sides facing. Referring to pattern trace heart shape onto wrong side of one piece.

2. Machine-stitch wallpaper layers together along traced line, leaving 2" opening at center top.

3. Using scalloped shears, trim away excess wallpaper, cutting ¼" from stitching.

4. Spray-paint both sides, allowing one side to dry completely before spraying second side.

5. Using transfer paper, transfer design onto surface of heart, Referring to photo, paint in a folk style; let dry. Add a coating of spray-on sealer or antique finish if desired.

6. Punch hole in center top of each lobe of heart; thread cording through and tie in a loop. Tuck netting into heart. ●

Stitching Line

"Country at Heart" Sign

Sift through your stash of old buttons to dress up this super design — great for sharing with the kids!

Design by Debbie Rines

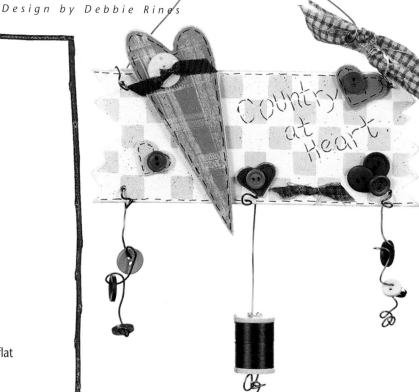

Materials

- Aleene's All-Purpose Primer by Duncan Enterprises
- Aleene's Satin Varnish #EN 102 by Duncan Enterprises
- Aleene's Stencil Medium #EN 115 by Duncan Enterprises
- Aleene's Premium Coat acrylic paints by Duncan Enterprises:
  Deep mauve #OC 104
  Dusty blue #OC 153
  Black #OC 176
  Ivory #OC 179
  Colonial blue #OC 219
  Oatmeal #OC 220
- Aleene's Thick Designer Tacky Glue by Duncan Enterprises
- Paintbrushes: ¾" flat, ½" rake and #10 flat
- Cosmetic sponge
- Spattering brush
- 7" x 2¾" wooden sign from Provo Craft
- 4¾" x 1¾" primitive wooden heart from Provo Craft
- Woodsies wooden hearts from Forster Inc.:
  1⅛" x ⅞"
  2 (⅞" x ¾")
- ½"-square checkerboard stencil
- Permanent black fine-point marking pen
- Fabric scraps
- Assorted buttons
- Small wooden spool of thread
- 19-gauge black wire
- Needle-nose pliers
- Wire cutters
- Fine sandpaper
- Pencil

Project Note

Refer to photo throughout.

Instructions

1. Using ¾" flat brush, seal all wooden pieces with primer; let dry. Sand.

2. Using ¾" flat brush, base-coat sign with ivory paint; base-coat primitive heart and 1⅛" heart with dusty blue; base-coat one of the smallest hearts with colonial blue and the other with deep mauve. Let all pieces dry; sand edges.

3. Mix oatmeal paint and stencil medium according to manufacturer's directions; using cosmetic sponge, stencil checks on sign.

4. Using spattering brush, spatter sign lightly with black paint.

5. Using rake brush and colonial blue paint, paint plaid lines on primitive heart; let dry.

6. Using ¾" brush, coat all wooden pieces with satin varnish. Let dry completely.

7. Using marking pen, write "Country at Heart" on sign.

8. Cut one piece of wire for hanger and three other lengths for suspending buttons and spool; coil around pencil and kink with pliers as desired. Thread hanger through holes in top corners of sign; tie two fabric bows around hanger. Suspend spool from one shorter piece and buttons from others; hang from holes along bottom of sign.

9. Glue hearts to sign and buttons to hearts. Glue knotted fabric bows to sign and buttons as desired. ✱

Fantastic Frames

A bit of creative "aging" gives the impression that these homey designs have stood the test of time — just like the warm sentiments they salute.

Designs by Bonnie Stephens

Hugs and Kisses Frame

Materials

- 6" x 8" chalkboard from D&CC
- 3¾" rusty tin star from D&CC
- 4 (1½") wooden primitive star cutouts from Woodworks
- Aleene's oak stain #AW 105 by Duncan Enterprises
- Aleene's Premium-Coat acrylic paints by Duncan Enterprises:
  Deep peach #OC 116
  Beige #OC 182
  Yellow ochre #OC 184
- Aleene's Decoupage, matte finish, by Duncan Enterprises
- Aleene's Thick Designer Tacky Glue by Duncan Enterprises

- ¾" flat paintbrush
- 6" x 8" unbleached muslin
- 1"-wide torn strips of country-check fabrics:
  10" country green check
  8" country blue check
  10" and 8" barn red check
  Small strip of either color
- Black fine-point permanent marking pen
- Fine sandpaper
- Paper towels
- Wire for hanger
- Needle-nose pliers
- Drill with small bit
- Pencil

Hugs & Kisses

Project Notes

Refer to photo throughout.

Instructions

1. Using ¾" flat brush, apply oak stain to frame of chalkboard; wipe off excess with paper towels.

2. Paint center of chalkboard with beige paint.

3. Squirt a small amount of deep peach paint into a small bowl of water; mix well. Immerse muslin in bowl; squeeze out excess liquid and lay flat to dry.

4. Apply decoupage to painted portion of chalkboard and to wrong side of stained muslin; lay muslin on chalkboard. Apply more decoupage to top of muslin and smooth with fingers; let dry.

5. Apply decoupage to top of chalkboard frame and backs of fabric strips. Place strips on top of frame and smooth with fingers. Apply another coat of decoupage to top of fabric; let dry.

6. Using ¾" flat brush, apply a small amount of yellow ochre paint to tin star; let dry.

7. Using fine-point marking pen, draw running stitch around star near edge. Tie strip of fabric in a knot; glue to top of tin star and glue star to chalkboard as shown.

8. Using ¾" flat brush, paint wooden stars yellow ochre and let dry; sand edges. Using fine-point marking pen, draw running stitch around edges of stars. Glue wooden stars in corners of frame.

9. Using fine-point marking pen, draw "running stitch" around edge of muslin inside frame, and write "HUGS AND KISSES STARS FOR WISHES" in running-stitch style.

10. Drill two holes in top of frame. For hanger, coil wire around pencil and kink with pliers as desired. Thread hanger through holes in frame from back to front. Coil wire to hold in place.

When Friends Meet

Project Notes

Refer to photo throughout.

Instructions

1. Using ¾" flat brush, apply oak stain to frame of chalkboard; wipe off excess with paper towels.

2. Paint center of chalkboard with beige paint.

3. Squirt a small amount of deep peach paint into a small bowl of water; mix well. Immerse muslin in bowl; squeeze out excess liquid and lay flat to dry.

4. Apply decoupage to painted portion of chalkboard

When Friends Meet Frame

Materials

- 6" x 8" chalkboard from D&CC
- 2" x 3" rusty heart from D&CC
- 4 (1⅜" x 1⅛") wooden heart cutouts from Woodworks
- Aleene's oak stain #AW 105 by Duncan Enterprises
- Aleene's Premium-Coat acrylic paints by Duncan Enterprises:
  Deep mauve #OC 104
  Deep peach #OC 116
  Beige #OC 182
- Aleene's Decoupage, matte finish, by Duncan Enterprises
- Aleene's Thick Designer Tacky Glue by Duncan Enterprises
- ¾" flat paintbrush
- 6" x 8" unbleached muslin
- 1"-wide torn strips of country-check fabrics:
  10" and 8" country green check
  10" and 8" barn red check
  Small strips of either color
- Black fine-point permanent marking pen
- Fine sandpaper
- Paper towels
- Wire for hanger
- Needle-nose pliers
- Drill with small bit

and to wrong side of stained muslin; lay muslin on chalkboard. Apply more decoupage to top of muslin and smooth with fingers; let dry.

5. Using ¾" flat brush, paint wooden hearts deep mauve and let dry; sand edges.

6. Apply decoupage to top of chalkboard frame and backs of fabric strips. Place strips on top of frame and smooth with fingers. Apply another coat of decoupage to top of fabric; let dry.

7. Glue wooden hearts in corners of frame. Tie small strip of fabric in a knot; glue to top of tin heart and glue heart to chalkboard as shown.

8. Using fine-point marking pen, draw "running stitch" around edge of muslin inside frame, and write "WHEN FRIENDS MEET HEARTS WARM" in running-stitch style.

9. Drill two holes in top corners of frame. For hanger, coil wire around pencil and kink with pliers as desired. Thread hanger through holes in frame from back to front. Coil wire to hold in place. ●

Friendly Felt Beanbag Pets

Propped on a desk, posed on a shelf, draped comfortably over the corner of your computer monitor, these lovable critters are comfortable anywhere—and full of beans!

Designs by Beth Wheeler

Materials

Both Projects

- Rainbow Felt Classics from Kunin Felt:
  2 (9" x 12") pieces pirate green #476
  1 (9" x 12") piece lime #494
  2 (9" x 12") pieces graystone #J65
- Matching sewing threads
- Sewing machine (optional)
- Hand-sewing needle
- Black pearl cotton or embroidery floss
- Black buttons:
  3 (⅛") and 5 (¼") ball-shaped
  2 (⅛") flat round buttons
- Red pony bead
- 10" cream or white satin rat-tail cord
- Polyester doll pellets or dried beans
- Small amount of polyester fiberfill

Froggy

Project Notes

Refer to photo throughout.

Instructions

1. Fold pirate green felt in half; referring to patterns (pages 152 and 153), cut two frogs from pirate green. Cut one tummy from lime.

2. Using black pearl cotton and hand-sewing needle, stitch a smile on one frog; by hand or machine, stitch tummy to this frog, stitching very close to edge of lime felt. With needle and black pearl cotton, sew running stitch down center of frog's lime tummy, adding an X for belly button.

3. Lay body pieces together, wrong sides facing. Stitching very close to edge, sew frogs together around periphery by machine or hand, leaving top of head open for stuffing.

4. Fill legs with pellets so they are squishy, not firm. Using hand-sewing needle and black pearl cotton, sew running stitch across tops of legs, under tummy, as indicated on pattern.

5. Fill frog's arms with pellets just until limbs are squishy; stitch across arms with black pearl cotton as indicated on pattern.

6. Fill tummy with pellets and fiberfill until squishy; with hand-sewing needle and black pearl cotton, stitch running stitch across neckline.

7. Stuff head firmly with fiberfill. Sew opening closed with green thread.

8. Using black thread, sew ¼" ball buttons in place for eyes and belly button; add flat buttons for nostrils.

Mousie

Project Notes

Refer to photo throughout.

Instructions

1. Referring to patterns (pages 152 and 153), cut two mice and two ears from graystone felt.

2. Using black pearl cotton and hand-sewing needle, stitch mouth and whiskers on one mouse and sew running stitch down center of mouse's tummy, adding an X for belly button.

3. Fold a small pleat in base of each ear; stitch through pleat using hand-sewing needle and matching sewing thread.

4. Lay body pieces together, wrong sides facing, and sandwiching bases of ears between body halves. Stitching very close to edge, sew mouse together around periphery by machine or hand, leaving top of head open for stuffing.

5. Fill legs with pellets so they are squishy, not firm. Using hand-sewing needle and black pearl cotton, sew running stitch across tops of legs to define bottom of tummy, as indicated on pattern.

6. Fill mouse's arms with pellets just until limbs are squishy; stitch across arms with black pearl cotton as indicated on pattern.

7. Fill tummy with pellets and fiberfill until squishy; with hand-sewing needle and black pearl cotton, stitch running stitch across neckline.

8. Stuff head firmly with fiberfill. Sew opening closed with gray thread.

9. Using black thread, sew smaller ball buttons in place for eyes and mouth; sew larger ball buttons in place for nose and belly button.

10. Slip pony bead over end of satin rat-tail cord; knot each end of cord. Stitch cord at base of mouse using hand-sewing needle and gray thread. ●

Scrub-a-Dub-Dub!

Whatever your personal housework philosophy, you'll get a giggle from this hardworking miss who finds herself up to her knees in the family suds and duds.

Design by Rochelle Norris

Materials

- 6" tin washtub
- Wooden shapes from Woodworks:
  2½" wooden egg #FF-E200
  1 pair mitten hands #CO-9327
- Wooden 4-piece clothesline set #5737 from Miller Woodcrafts
- Bamboo skewers: 4" and 2 (6")
- 2 (10") ¼"-diameter wooden dowels
- Americana acrylic paints from DecoArt:
  Titanium (snow) white #DA1
  Hi-lite flesh #DA24
  Mocha #DA60
  Lamp (ebony) black #DA67
  Desert sand #DA77
  Uniform blue #DA86
  French grey blue #DA98
  Cherry red #DA159
  Light buttermilk #DA164
  Napa red #DA165
  Deep midnight blue #DA166
  Payne's grey #DA167
  Black plum #DA172
  DeLane's dark flesh #DA181
  French vanilla #DA184
  Light French blue #DA185
- Golden Taklon paintbrushes from Loew-Cornell:
  #2–#12 shader or flat brushes
- ¾" wash brush
  10/0 liner brush
  #2, #6 and #8 fabric stencil brushes
- Waxed paper
- Stencils:
  ⅜" checkerboard pattern
  ½" checkerboard pattern
- Double-ended stylus
- Rose cosmetic blusher
- Cotton swab
- Pens from Sakura of America:
  .02, .03 and .05 black Pigma pens
  Identi Pen black marking pen
- 8" x 10" white poster board
- Torn 12" x 17" print fabric rectangle for shirt
- Torn coordinating fabric scraps, including unbleached muslin
- Matching heavy-duty threads and hand-sewing needle
- Polyester fiberfill
- Coordinating ⅛"-wide satin ribbon
- Red doll hair
- Fine jute twine
- Drill with ⅟16", ³⁄32" and ¼" bits
- Hot-glue gun and glue sticks
- Block of plastic foam 2" thick to fit in washtub

Project Notes

Refer to Project Notes for "Special Mum" on page 35.

Refer to patterns on page 154 for painting and finishing details.

Head & Hands

1. Refer to Head & Hands instructions for "Special Mum," page 35, substituting wooden egg for ball, and base-coating head and hands with mocha; highlight with hi-lite flesh and shade with DeLane's dark flesh.

2. Referring to Fig. 1 (page 154), finish hands and face as for "Special Mum" except do not stipple cheeks.

Additional Painting and Finishing

1. *Jumper:* Base-coat with French grey blue; highlight with light French blue; shade with uniform blue. Using a dry paintbrush and very little titanium white paint, paint horizontal and vertical strokes across painted jumper. Dip small end of stylus in French vanilla; dot on clusters of three dots. Dip large point of stylus in uniform blue and dot on buttons. With small brush and Payne's gray, paint bow at neckline. Add outlining details with Pigma pen.

2. *Pants:* Base-coat with deep midnight blue; highlight with uniform blue; shade with Payne's grey. Using a dry paintbrush and very little titanium white paint,

paint horizontal and vertical strokes across painted pants. Using a fine paintbrush and French vanilla, add outlines and stitch details. Dip large point of stylus in Payne's gray; dot on button closure at waistband.

3. *Sign:* Base-coat with light buttermilk; highlight with titanium white; shade with desert sand. Using ½" stencil, add checks to quilt sign, alternating French vanilla and French grey blue. Using Pigma pen, draw dot-dash pattern around top and sides of sign. Add lettering with Identi Pen, using fine tip to write "My house was clean last week. Sorry you missed it" and the broad tip to add dots to ends of lines in letters.

4. *Shirt:* Base-coat with Napa red; highlight with cherry red and shade with black plum. Using French vanilla and ⅜" stencil, add checks. Using dry paintbrush and very little titanium white paint, paint horizontal and vertical strokes across shirt. Using small stylus point dipped in uniform blue, add dots between checks. Dipping small stylus point in Napa red, dot buttons down front.

Clothing

1. Referring to instructions for "Special Mum," follow steps 1–7 in instructions for "Clothing." Use patterns for poster-board shirt and fabric shirt on pages 157 and 158.

2. *Pocket:* Tear 3" x 4" scrap of coordinating fabric; fold over one 3" edge 1"; fold back ½" to make pocket flap. Hand-stitch pocket to front of shirt. Tear 4" scrap of muslin; fold and insert into pocket.

3. Tie ribbon in bow; glue at neckline.

Hair & Mop

1. For bangs, wrap two strands of hair six times around a 2" section of cardboard; cut along one edge and glue cut ends to top of head.

2. For hair, wrap two strands of hair 12 times around a 12" section of cardboard; cut along both edges and tie strands in center with another strand of hair. Glue, centered to lower back of head. Pull hair to top of head and tie together with a small fabric scrap. Spot-glue hair as needed to hold it in place.

3. For mop, tear 12 (4") strips of muslin. Referring to Fig. 2 and Fig. 3, lay strips together; insert ¼"-diameter dowel; tie strips to dowel with heavy-duty thread. Fold strips over so all ends are together; wrap more thread around tops of strips and knot. Spot-glue to hold in place.

Assembly

1. Drill two holes in top corners of jumper, shirt and pants. Thread a 20" length of jute twine through holes in clothes and thread ends through holes in hands; knot twine to secure.

2. Glue plastic foam into washtub; cover foam with fiberfill "suds." Apply glue to end of doll dowel and insert through fiberfill into foam base.

3. Glue 4" skewer to back of quilt sign; insert through foam into washtub. Glue mop in place, tying handle to doll's hand with heavy-duty thread. ✦

Last-Minute Gifts

All of us occasionally find ourselves needing a personal gift in a hurry. With this collection of easy-to-make crafts, you'll find the perfect gift for any occasion!

Birdhouse Flowerpots

Painted flowerpots like these make beautiful settings for plants, of course, but they're also excellent "gift boxes" for your favorite gardener, loaded with garden gloves, seed packets, gardener's hand soap, etc. Use our samples as guidelines, and let your creative flair take over!

Design by Doxie Keller for DecoArt

Materials

- Terra-cotta or plastic flowerpot
- Patio paint from DecoArt:
  Fern green #DCP3
  Pine green #DCP4
  Sunshine yellow #DCP6
  Geranium red #DCP7
  Pot o' gold #DCP11
  Daisy cream #DCP15
  Wrought iron black #DCP21
  Light eucalyptus green #DCP23
  Clear coat #DCP24
- Paintbrushes
- Small artist's sponge (optional)
- Low-tack masking tape (optional)

Project Notes

It is not necessary to seal the pots before painting, but you *must* cover all edges, rims, drain holes, etc., with paint.

Paints may be applied with brushes, a small piece of sponge, or both.

If you want to thin paints for artistic effects, use *only* clear coat, *not* water.

Allow paint to dry between coats.

Clean brushes, sponges and hands frequently with soap and water; patio paint is durable and more difficult to remove than other paints. But remember to paint only with a completely dry brush or sponge; water is the enemy of patio paint!

Instructions

1. Wipe any dust or dirt from pot; make sure pot is completely dry.

2. Referring to pattern (page 28) and photo, base-coat outside of pot rim with daisy cream and outside of pot, including bottom, with light eucalyptus green. Base-coat inside of pot with pot o' gold. Remember to make sure that all edges, including drainage holes, are covered with paint.

3. *Left birdhouse:* paint roof with daisy cream and birdhouse with a mixture of pine and fern greens. Paint openings in birdhouse with daisy cream.

4. *Center birdhouse:* Paint roof black; birdhouse is a shaded blend of daisy cream, sunshine yellow and geranium red, beginning with lightest color at bottom of birdhouse and blending to darkest color at top. Paint openings black.

5. *Right birdhouse:* Base-coat heart shape with daisy cream; add geranium red stripes and black opening.

6. *Flowers:* Blend a combination of daisy cream, sunshine yellow and geranium red. Paint centers sunshine yellow; add dots of black around centers.

7. *Leaves and stems:* Paint using a combination of fern green, pine green and sunshine yellow.

8. Outline all components and add birdhouse posts with black. Add tendrils and tiny leaves using greens

and highlighting with daisy cream. Speckle surface of painted pot very lightly with pot o' gold.

9. *Rim:* Paint a checkerboard pattern of fern green over daisy cream, using low-tack masking tape to mask off squares, if desired. Remove tape promptly after painting. Outline squares in black, if desired. Or, paint rims a solid color.

10. When painting is complete, coat all surfaces with clear coat. No other surface finish is needed.

Birdhouse Flowerpots

Valentine Heart Box

A ready-made papier-mâché box makes this project as quick as it is attractive!
It's a lovely way to present homemade cookies or your beloved's favorite chocolates.

Design by Angie Wilhite

Materials

- 9" x 9" x 5" heart-shaped papier-mâché box with lid
- Construction paper: 2 sheets each red and white
- Scallop and ripple paper-edging scissors
- 25" piece ⅛"-wide white satin ribbon
- Ready-made fabric yo-yos:
  2 (3") and 2 (2") brown star print
  6 (1") tan homespun
  4 (2") and 2 (1") red pin dot
  4 (1") white
- Red sewing thread and needle
- 4 (7mm) round black movable eyes
- Glue stick
- Fabric glue
- Jewel glue

Instructions

1. Cut three 1" x 11" strips from red construction paper; edge with ripple scissors.

2. Referring to patterns (page 155), cut paper hearts as indicated. Edge hearts with scallop scissors.

3. Cut ribbon into five 5" pieces; tie each in a bow.

4. Using fabric glue and referring to photo throughout, assemble boy bear by gluing 2" brown star yo-yo to top edge of 3" brown star yo-yo. Glue two 1" tan home-spun yo-yos to back of 2" brown star yo-yo for ears. Glue 1" tan homespun yo-yo on top of 2" brown star yo-yo, with their bottom edges even.

5. Using jewel glue, glue two eyes to face. Make bow tie by sewing a gathering stitch from one edge of a 1"

red pin-dot yo-yo to the other edge; pull thread tight and wrap once around yo-yo. Tack thread in back. Using fabric glue, glue bow to bear's chin.

6. Repeat steps 4 and 5 to make girl bear, except glue bow over left ear.

7. Using fabric glue, glue a white 1" yo-yo to each 2" red pin-dot yo-yo.

8. Using glue stick and referring to photo, glue large white paper heart to center of lid; center large red paper heart over it and glue. Glue small white heart to large red heart, and small red heart over small white heart. Glue yo-yo bears to large red heart.

9. Using glue stick through step 10, glue red paper strips around edge of lid, overlapping ends slightly.

10. Glue medium white hearts around sides of box, spacing them evenly, about 3½" apart. Center and glue medium red hearts over medium white hearts.

11. Using fabric glue, glue white-on-red yo-yo combinations to box between paper hearts. Referring to photo, glue ribbon bow to small heart on lid, and to each red heart on side of box.

"Love Me, Love My Cats"

Whether your taste runs to pedigreed Persians or anything that purrs, this colorful painted plaque lets the world know that felines come first with you!

Design by Delores F. Ruzicka

Materials

- 10" x 12" pine stock
- Ceramcoat acrylic paints from Delta Technical Coatings Inc.:
  Antique gold #2002
  Georgia clay #2097
  Woodland night green #2100
  Light ivory #2401
  Santa Fe rose #2496
  Black #2506
- American Painter paintbrushes from Loew-Cornell:
  Series #2550 ½" wash brush
  Series #4000 #3 round brush
  Series #4300 #8
- Walnut gel wood stain #53 208 from Delta Technical Coatings Inc.
- Satin-finish wood sealer
- 3 torn ⅜" x 8" cotton fabric strips in colors/patterns of your choice
- 18" fine jute twine
- Tacky craft glue
- Band saw or scroll saw
- Sandpaper
- Tack cloth
- Drill with ⅛" bit

Project Notes

Let paint dry before applying overlaying or adjacent colors.

Refer to photo throughout.

Instructions

1. Referring to pattern (page 156), cut design from stock using band saw or scroll saw. Sand edges until smooth; wipe off sawdust with tack cloth.

2. Drill ⅛" holes for hanging where indicated on plaque.

3. Using #8 brush, paint left cat antique gold, center cat light ivory and right cat black. Paint sign on which cats sit Georgia clay. Two coats may be necessary for thorough coverage.

4. Using #3 round brush through step 7, paint details on cats: Paint noses and insides of ears with Santa Fe rose.

5. Paint black eyes on gold and light ivory cats. Paint smaller ovals of woodland night green on top of black eyes; paint woodland night green eyes on black cat. Using black, draw a very narrow line down center of green ovals on all cats, and add eyelashes at eyes' bottom outer corners on gold and light ivory cats. Using light ivory, add outlines and eyelashes to black cat's eyes, and add tiny highlight dots at tops of all cats' eyes.

6. Using black for light ivory and gold cats and light ivory for black cat, add whiskers and "freckles," vertical mouth lines, details to ears, and outlines of legs and cats.

7. Using light ivory, paint "Love Me…. Love My Cats" on plaque.

8. Thin a small amount of walnut gel stain with water; shade cats' outlines and around their legs. Stain sides and back of plaque with gel stain, if desired.

9. Apply sealer to plaque using ½" wash brush.

10. Tie twine through holes for hanger. Tie fabric strips in bows; glue one to each cat's neckline. ❦

Country Angel Frame

Photos are wonderful keepsakes, forever freezing in time a special occasion or the faces of loved ones.

The next time you share a special photo with someone, enclose it in this sweet, country-style frame.

Design by Bonnie Stephens

Project Notes

Let stain, paint and varnish dry before applying overlaying or adjacent colors or proceeding with assembly.

Refer to photo throughout for placement.

Staining & Painting

1. Using sponge applicator, apply whitewash to frame. Wipe off excess with paper towel. Apply a small amount of oak stain; wipe lightly with a paper towel.

2. Spatter frame lightly with a small amount of thinned black paint.

3. Paint dusty sage diagonal stripes on frame using ½" flat brush. Using fine-point marking pen, draw dashed-line pattern around edge of frame and along both sides of dusty sage stripes.

4. Apply a coat of matte varnish to frame using a ¾" flat brush, if desired.

5. Using ¾" flat brush, paint wooden heart and circles

Continued on page 43

Materials

- Small frame #3591 from Walnut Hollow
- 1½"-diameter wooden ball knob, or wooden ball with thin slice cut from one side
- 5½"-wide rusty tin wings from D&CC
- 1½" flat wooden heart from Woodworks
- Woodsies wooden cutouts from Forster Inc.:
  3 (¾"-diameter) circles
  6 (⅞") leaves
- Aleene's wood-finishing products by Duncan Enterprises:
  Whitewash stain #AW 102
  Oak stain #AW 105
  Matte varnish #EN 107
- Aleene's Premium Coat acrylic paints by Duncan Enterprises:
  Dusty sage #OC 135

Black #OC 176
Blush #OC 183
Burgundy #OC 186
Primrose #OC 213

- Paintbrushes:
  ½" flat
  ¾" flat
  Spattering brush
- Sponge applicator
- Stylus
- Black fine-point permanent marking pen
- Aleene's Platinum Bond #7800 glue by Duncan Enterprises
- Paper towels
- Dried Spanish moss
- ¾"-wide fabric strip

Rusty Tin Angel Ornament

Don't let her "rusty" wings fool you — this little angel is definitely up to the task! She's easy to craft and fun to make, from her shredded brown paper hair to her golden "halo."

Design by Delores F. Ruzicka

Materials
- 5½" rusty tin wings from D&CC
- 1½"-tall wooden half-egg
- Crafter's Pick Ultimate Tacky Glue by API
- Crinkled brown shredded paper
- American Painter series #4300 size 6 paintbrush from Loew-Cornell
- Black fine-point permanent marking pen
- Ceramcoat acrylic paints from Delta Technical Coatings Inc.: Island coral #2433 Santa's flesh #2472 White #2505
- 1" gold ring
- 12" piece gold cord

Project Notes
Let paint dry before painting adjacent or overlaying colors.

Refer to photo throughout.

Instructions
1. Paint the wooden half-egg with Santa's flesh paint; blend in island coral for cheeks. When dry, draw eyes, using permanent black marking pen. Add a very small white highlight to each eye and cheeks.

2. Glue wooden head to tin wings; glue on shredded paper for hair and gold ring for halo; let dry.

3. Glue loop of gold cord to center back of wings for hanger.

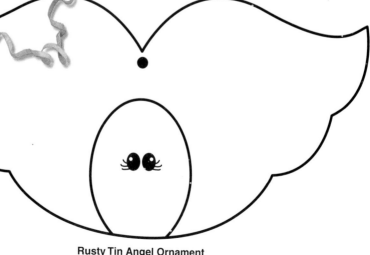

Rusty Tin Angel Ornament

Materials

- 4"-diameter x 2¼"-deep terra-cotta seed pan
- Wooden shapes from Woodworks:
  2½" wooden ball #RB-2500
  3 (¾") wooden finishing buttons #BB-0750
  1 pair mitten hands #CO-9327
  3½" ribbon #CO-9924
  Bow #CO-5625
- Bamboo skewers: 4" and 2 (6")
- 10" (¼"-diameter) wooden dowel
- Americana acrylic paints from DecoArt:
  Titanium (snow) white #DA1
  Hi-lite flesh #DA24
  Raspberry #DA28
  Lamp (ebony) black #DA67
  Uniform blue #DA86
  French grey blue #DA98
  Cranberry wine #DA112
  Hauser medium green #DA132
  Base flesh #DA136
  DeLane's dark flesh #DA181
  Light French blue #DA185
- Golden Taklon paintbrushes from Loew-Cornell:
  #2–#12 shader or flat brushes
  ¾" wash brush
  10/0 liner brush
- Waxed paper
- Double-ended stylus
- Rose cosmetic blusher
- Cotton swab
- Pens from Sakura of America:
  .02, .03 and .05 Pigma black marking pens
  Identi Pen black marking pen
- 8" x 10" white poster board
- Torn 12" x 17" print fabric rectangle for shirt
- Torn fabric strips in assorted coordinating prints:
  2 (3" x 12")
  2 (2½" x 10")
  2 (2" x 8")
- Matching heavy-duty threads and hand-sewing needle
- Polyester fiberfill
- 12" piece coordinating ⅛"-wide satin ribbon
- 1 package auburn curly doll hair
- Dried Spanish moss
- 24" piece 20-gauge wire
- 4 (½") flat buttons
- Drill with 1⁄16", 3⁄32" and ¼" bits
- Hot-glue gun and glue sticks
- Block of plastic foam 2" thick to fit in seed pan
- Ball-point ink pen
- Pencil

Special Mum

Friendly little smiles bloom all over this clever country-style design. If you'd like, add as many "flower babies" as you wish to represent your own mom's precious "sprouts."

Design by Rochelle Norris

Project Notes

Follow these general guidelines for painting:

Base-coating: Paint piece, covering it as evenly as possible. Several thin coats of paint are better than one thick, heavy coat.

Highlighting: Highlight each piece along top edge and left side. Dip brush in water and blot on paper towel. Dip one corner of brush (about one-third) into the paint; run brush back and forth on waxed paper in the same spot to distribute paint evenly in brush. Slowly and evenly, pull brush along area to be highlighted.

Shading: Shade each piece along bottom edge and right side, using same technique as for highlighting.

When a specific pen size is not indicated for outlining or adding details with Pigma pens, select the pen width according to the application—larger for outlining, smaller for more delicate lines and detail work.

Use the Identi Pen for the larger lettering with dots on the ends of the lines: Write the letters with the narrower end and add the dots with the larger end.

Let paint dry between applications unless otherwise instructed.

Refer to photo throughout.

Head & Hands

1. Drill hole in bottom of wooden ball head with ¼" bit. Apply glue to end of ¼"-diameter dowel; insert into head. Referring to Fig. 1, drill hole in base of each hand with ³⁄₃₂" bit; drill hole through front of each hand with ¹⁄₁₆" bit.

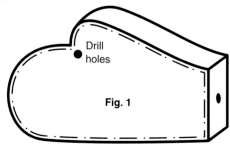

Drill holes

Fig. 1

2. Base-coat head and hands with base flesh; highlight with hi-lite flesh; shade with DeLane's dark flesh.

3. Referring to Fig. 2, dot on eyes with large end of stylus dipped in black paint. When dry, use cotton swab to brush cheeks with cosmetic blusher. Using DeLane's dark flesh, lightly stipple cheeks. Using .02 Pigma pen, draw smile.

Fig. 2

4. Using Pigma pen, add dot-dash outline around fronts of hands.

5. Hot-glue each hand to blunt end of a 6" skewer, inserting skewer in holes in base of hands.

Additional Painting & Finishing

1. *Sign:* Base-coat ribbon with light French blue; highlight with white; shade with French grey blue.

2. Using fine tip of Identi Pen, write "You're a Very Special Mum" on sign; add border around edge with Pigma pen. Dot circles on ends of lines in letters with large tip of Identi Pen. Speckle sign lightly with titanium white.

3. *Seed Pan:* Base-coat rim of seed pan with French grey blue; highlight with light French blue; shade with uniform blue. Base-coat base of seed pan with raspberry.

4. Referring to Fig. 3, base-coat evenly spaced flowers around rim with raspberry; highlight with hi-lite flesh; shade with cranberry wine.

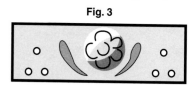

Fig. 3

5. Using hi-lite flesh, speckle seed pan rim and base. Dip small end of stylus into light French blue and add groups of three dots between flowers on rim. Using Hauser medium green and small brush, paint comma-stroke leaves. Further define flowers with a few strokes with Pigma pen.

6. *Bow:* Base-coat with French grey blue; highlight with light French blue; shade with uniform blue. Speckle lightly with white.

7. Dip small end of stylus into raspberry and add groups of three dots to bow. Add details with Pigma pen.

Clothing

1. Referring to pattern (page 157), trace shirt onto poster board; draw fold lines with ball-point pen, pressing down firmly. Cut out. Using sharp end of scissors, poke hole where indicated. Fold sides of shirt down along lines.

2. Fold torn 12" x 17" rectangle into quarters, right sides facing; pin layers together. Referring to pattern (page 158), cut one shirt from folded fabric, positioning shoulder and center seams along folds and sleeve opening along torn edge. Cut off corner at neck to make neck opening.

3. Unfold shirt (Fig. 4). Fold shirt halves together, right sides facing (Fig. 5), and sew up sides and under arms.

Fig. 4

Fig. 5

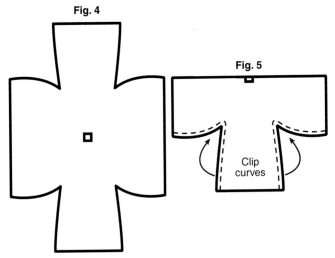

Clip curves; turn shirt right side out.

4. Sew gathering stitch around each sleeve opening ½" from edge, beginning and ending at seam. Sew a gathering stitch around bottom of shirt 1" from edge of fabric, starting and ending at center front.

5. Insert folded poster-board shirt inside fabric shirt. Insert dowel with head through holes in shirts, fitting head snugly against poster board (Fig. 6). Squirt glue along dowel and across bottom of poster-board shirt; press together, making sure dowel is centered and head rests against top fold and faces forward.

6. Insert skewers with hands into open ends of poster-board sleeves; hands should extend 1" beyond edge of poster-board sleeve. Hot-glue skewers to poster board. Pull threads at sleeve openings, gathering sleeves evenly around hands; knot threads. Spot-glue sleeves to hold them in place. Clip thread ends 1" from knot.

7. Insert small amount of polyester fiberfill in bottom half of shirt front. Pull gathering thread at bottom of shirt closed; knot and tie thread ends in a bow.

Fig. 6

8. Glue painted bow at Mum's neckline.

Hair

1. Cut 18 (11") strands of hair (do not stretch hair while measuring); glue, centered, over top of head.

2. Cut 18 (8") strands of hair; glue to top of head, leaving 1½" in front for bangs and the rest hanging down the back.

3. Repeat both steps until all hair is used; trim to desired length. Lift hair and run a bead of glue around back of head from ear to ear; quickly lay hair into glue. Pull hair together at back and tie with ribbon.

Flowers

1. *Add face to each of the wooden finishing buttons:* Dip small end of stylus in black paint and dot on eyes. Draw smile with Pigma pen. Use cotton swab to lightly apply cosmetic blusher for cheeks.

2. *Fabric rosettes:* Referring to Fig. 7, fold one of the torn fabric strips in half, right sides facing and matching short ends; sew ends together, leaving ⅜" seam allowance. Open seam allowance; press flat.

Fig. 7

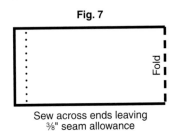

Sew across ends leaving
⅜" seam allowance

3. Fold loop in half, wrong sides facing (Fig. 8), and sew a gathering stitch around top ⅛" from edges. Pull thread ends to gather fabric and press flat to make a rosette; knot thread ends. Repeat with remaining strips.

4. Glue rosettes together in pairs to make three flowers: one small rosette made from an 8" strip atop medium rosette made from a 10" strip; one medium rosette atop large rosette made from a 12" strip, and remaining small rosette atop remaining large rosette. Glue wooden button face to center of each flower. Glue 4" skewer to back of smallest flower.

Fig. 8

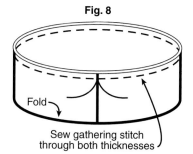

Fold

Sew gathering stitch
through both thicknesses

Assembly

1. *Hot-glue back of sign to center of wire:* Apply a large dot of glue to each end of sign on back; lay wire into glue, and press ½" button into glue over wire. Using same method, hot-glue a flower to wire on each side of sign. Thread wire through holes in hands; twist wire ends together and coil around pencil.

2. Glue plastic foam in bottom of seed pan; cover foam with Spanish moss and spot-glue. Apply glue to end of doll dowel; insert through Spanish moss and secure in foam base.

3. Apply glue to end of skewer on back of smallest flower; stick into foam base to left of Mum.

Materials
- 5½" x 7" piece corrugated cardboard
- Lightweight cardboard:
  5½" x 7" piece
  1½" x 3½" strip
- Clear-drying craft cement
- Frame decorations: stamps, buttons, coins, twine, small shells, keys, etc.
- Sharp craft knife
- Aleene's Tacky Glue by Duncan Enterprises
- 3½" x 5" photograph

Collage Frame

Commemorate a special occasion and create a one-of-a-kind gift by presenting a favorite photo in this super-easy picture frame. The decorations you select will give the frame your exclusive design — and create a cherished personal momento.

Design by Helen L. Rafson

Project Notes
Adjust dimensions of the frame and the decorations to suit your photograph.

Instructions

1. Using craft knife, cut a 4¼" x 2¾" opening from center of corrugated cardboard for frame front.

2. Glue decorations to frame front as desired, using craft cement for metal items and tacky glue for other materials; lay frame flat to dry.

3. Apply a line of craft glue to 5½" x 7" lightweight cardboard about ¼" from top, left and bottom edges (right edge remains unglued so photo can be inserted); top with embellished frame front. Let dry completely.

4. Cut cardboard strip in half to make two 1½" x 1¾" pieces. Make stand for frame by gluing pieces together into a "V" along one 1½" edge; let dry completely. Then glue open end of V to back of frame at center bottom; let dry.

5. Insert photo through right edge of frame.

Country Cabin
Coasters & Hot Pad

Cabin-style decor is very popular, and these pieces make perfect accents for your cabin-style table. Just draw the pattern with an easy-to-use woodburning tool, and paint.

Design by Creative Chi

Materials

- 7½" round cork hot pad
- 4 (3¾") round cork coasters
- Woodburning tool with mini-flow point
- Designer cosmetic artist's paintbrush #4300 from Loew-Cornell
- Apple Barrel Indoor/Outdoor Gloss acrylic enamel paints from Plaid Enterprises Inc.:
  Purple velvet #20627
  Real red #20636
  Real yellow #20645
  Forest green #20649
  Real green #20651
  Real blue #20660
  Black #20662
  Coffee bean #20666

Coaster

Instructions

1. Referring to design patterns below, transfer designs to hot pad and coasters (see General Instructions, page 188).

2. Attach mini flow tip to woodburning tool; preheat. Burn design into cork, following pattern lines. Very little pressure is needed.

3. Thin paints slightly with water to form a wash of color. Paint center tree with real green and outer trees with forest green. Paint window with real yellow, door with real red, and cabin with coffee bean.

4. Paint mountains with a mixture of black and purple velvet, and paint rocks with a very light wash of black. Paint stream with real blue.

Hot Pad

Sunflower Photo Album

If you love the look of silk ribbon embroidery but don't want to commit to an enormous project, here's a perfect option! Using only two stitches, you can create a sunflower.

Design by Nancy Marshall

Instructions

1. Stamp design in center of fabric.

2. Following diagram and referring to stitch diagrams for Japanese Ribbon Stitch and French Knot, work orange petals first, then pale honey petals.

3. Stitch two rounds of brown French knots in center next to petals, and another cluster of brown French knots in very center of flower center. Fill in remaining portions of center with gold French knots.

4. Using cotton swab moistened in water, remove any remaining visible ink from stamped design. Trim fabric to 5" square with sunflower in center.

5. Round off corners of mounting board. Center stitched piece on board, wrapping excess neatly to back and gluing fabric in place.

Materials

- 5½" x 6½" fabric-covered photograph album
- 6" square of 32-count white Jobelan #862-0 from Wichelt Imports
- Comotion Sunflower Bloom rubber stamp #1935
- Tsukineko erasable fabric ink pad
- Bucilla silk embroidery ribbon:
  1 yard 7mm pale honey #503
  1 yard 7mm orange #522
  2¼ yards 4mm gold #668
  3½ yards 4mm brown #671
- Ribbon embroidery needle
- Embroidery hoop
- 14" piece brown maxi piping from Wrights
- 9" piece white 1"-wide grosgrain ribbon
- 3" square padded mounting board, or 3" square mounting board with glued-on batting
- Small piece of card stock
- Craft glue
- Cotton-tip swab

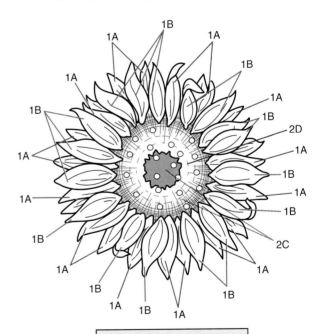

STITCHES
1 Japanese Ribbon Stitch
2 French Knot
COLORS/RIBBON
A 7mm orange #522
B 7mm pale honey #503
C 4mm brown #671
D 4mm gold #668
Color numbers given are for Bucilla silk embroidery ribbon.

6. Cut piping to fit around board edge plus 1". At each end, trim cord and turn in raw edge. Glue piping around board edge.

7. Center and glue a 9" piece of gold embroidery silk ribbon down center of grosgrain ribbon. Cut one end in points. Center and glue ribbon to album cover so front points are 1" above bottom edge and other end extends inside front cover.

8. Cut label from card stock; glue to inside cover, covering end of grosgrain ribbon. Glue stitched piece to album cover ¾" below top album edge.

French Knot

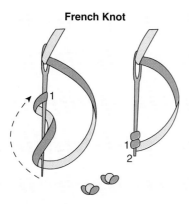

When embroidering with ribbon, both Single and Double French Knots can be used. They are worked more loosely than when using floss or yarn. This double version gives good results. Bring needle up at 1 and wrap ribbon twice around the shaft of the needle. Insert the point of the needle into fabric at 2, close to 1. Keep the working ribbon wrapped (not too tightly) around the needle as you pull needle through to back of fabric. Release the wrapping ribbon as knot is formed, and do not pull the knot too tightly. To make a Single French Knot, use only one wrap.

Japanese Ribbon Stitch

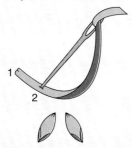

Bring your needle up at 1 and flatten the ribbon as it emerges through the fabric. Extend the ribbon just beyond the length of the stitch and insert needle through top of ribbon at 2. Pull ribbon gently through fabric and each side of the ribbon will curl toward the pierced point. Leave the curls showing by not pulling too tightly. This is also called an Inverted Straight Stitch or a Leaf Stitch and is usually worked with wide ribbon.

Dressed-up Hand Mirror

A recycled hand mirror takes on a whole new allure when it's given a fresh life with some colorful yo-yos.

D e s i g n   b y   M a r y   T .   C o s g r o v e

M a t e r i a l s

- Hand mirror with 6" round mirror
- 21 large pastel fabric yo-yos by Wimpole Street Creations
- Small pastel fabric yo-yo by Wimpole Street Creations
- Miniature Battenburg Assortment by Wimpole Street Creations
- Approximately 24" piece 1¼"-wide white Cluny lace
- Fabri-Tac fabric adhesive from Beacon Adhesives

P r o j e c t   N o t e

Refer to photo throughout for placement.

The number of yo-yos and amount of Cluny lace needed may vary with the size and shape of your mirror.

I n s t r u c t i o n s

1. Run a line of glue along the outside edge of the back of the mirror. Add Cluny lace.

2. Working counterclockwise, glue a row of 14 large yo-yos, overlapping them, along outer edge to cover seam of Cluny lace.

3. Glue a second row of six large yo-yos in the same manner; they should overlap the first row.

4. Add the last large yo-yo to center back of mirror; back of mirror should be completely covered.

5. Glue miniature Battenburg lace piece to center of yo-yos; glue small yo-yo in center of lace.

Cool CD Clock

A simple clock mechanism and funky ornaments of polymer clay turn a cast-off CD into an original work of art. When your kids see this, they'll want to make one for each of their friends!

Design by Margi Laurin

Materials

- Recycled or new blank CD
- Small amounts of polymer clay: red, yellow, turquoise, black, or colors of your choice
- Super glue or craft epoxy
- Clock mechanism
- Utility knife
- Waxed paper or baking parchment
- Cardboard
- Baking dish
- Black marking pen or masking tape

Project Notes

Before you begin, test the fit of the central clock pin through the center of the CD. If pin is too large, enlarge CD opening with utility knife until pin fits snugly.

Clean hands thoroughly before you begin working with a different color of clay to prevent color from transferring.

Tape a piece of waxed paper or parchment to a piece of cardboard and use it as your work surface.

Modeling Clay

1. Condition a walnut-size portion of each color clay by squeezing it with your hands until it is soft and pliable. (You may have to work it again just before using.)

2. Mix small amounts—no more than ⅛ block each—of red and turquoise to make purple. Mix red and yellow to make a medium orange.

3. Mold a disk of red about the size and thickness of a quarter (Fig. 1). Roll a long snake of turquoise and create a spiral on the red disk. Press in place gently.

Fig. 1

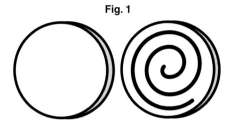

4. Using utility knife, cut a circle in the center of the disk that is big enough for the clock's central pin to fit through. Line baking sheet with parchment or waxed paper and place disk on it.

5. For the 12 o'clock position, mold a piece of orange into a ball the size of a small marble. Make a tiny snake of black and press gently in a coil in center, flattening piece slightly (Fig. 2). Place on prepared baking sheet.

Fig. 2

6. For the 3 o'clock position, make a similar size triangle of turquoise. Make some tiny black snakes and place them on triangle to form stripes (Fig. 3). Press gently. Place on prepared baking sheet.

Fig. 3

7. For the 6 o'clock position, mold a piece of yellow into a ball the size of a small marble. Add tiny dots of black clay (Fig. 4). Press gently. Place on prepared baking sheet.

Fig. 4

8. For the 9 o'clock position, make a square of purple; add tiny black stripes (Fig. 5); press gently and place on prepared baking sheet.

9. To indicate the other hours, make tiny logs of

different colors and cut each to about ¼" long (Fig. 6). Place on baking sheet.

10. Bake clay parts according to manufacturer's instructions; let cool completely.

Fig. 5

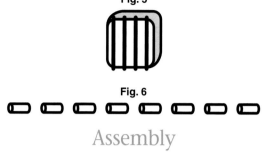

Fig. 6

Assembly

1. Using a ruler, mark locations for 12, 3, 6 and 9 o'clock on CD using black marker or bits of masking tape. Carefully glue clay markers in place.

2. Glue on tiny logs to represent other hours.

3. Glue on center disk, aligning hole with CD hole.

4. Assemble clock on CD following instructions on package. 🪨

Country Angel Frame
Continued from page 32

with burgundy; paint knob with blush; paint leaves with dusty sage.

6. Dip stylus tip in black paint and dot eyes onto painted knob. Paint cheeks using ½" flat brush and a small amount of primrose.

7. Add highlights to burgundy cherries with a touch of primrose. Using fine-point marking pen, add veins to dusty sage leaves.

Finishing & Assembly

1. Glue knob to center top edge of frame; glue a little dried Spanish moss to top of head for hair. Tie fabric strip in a simple knot; trim ends as desired and glue to hair.

2. Glue wings to top of frame under head; glue heart to wings. Glue cherries and leaves to surface of frame. 🪨

Teddy Bear Pocket Purse

Some little sweetie you know would go wild over this darling purse! You won't believe how simple it is to make from a pair of your old blue jeans.

Design by Janna Britton

Materials

- Leg and pocket from adult-size blue jeans
- Fiberfill
- About ⅛ cup polyester doll pellets
- Tulip slick dimensional paints from Duncan Enterprises: light brown, black, white and deep red
- Toothpick
- White sewing thread and needle
- Scrap of denim #J56 Rainbow Felt Classic from Kunin Felt
- 12" piece ¼"-wide red picot-edge satin ribbon
- 12" square red bandanna-print or gingham fabric
- Sewing machine with zigzag stitch

Instructions

1. Cut back pocket from jeans, cutting through both layers of fabric and trimming close to stitching on pocket. Zigzag-stitch across pocket's back top raw edge.

2. From leg fabric, cut 4" x 28" strip for purse strap. Fold in half lengthwise, wrong sides facing. Machine-sew seam down strip ⅝" from fold. Cut edges in ¼"-wide fringe, ending cuts ¼" from stitched line. Stitch strap ends to top back edge of pocket.

3. Referring to patterns (page 159), cut muzzle from denim felt and other teddy bear pieces from remaining leg fabric. Using ⅛" seam allowance and stitching with right sides of denim facing through step 5, stitch body fronts together along center edge. Stitch one head to body front and the other to body back.

4. Stitch ears together in pairs. Pin straight edges inside head where indicated; stitch head and body pieces together, leaving opening at bottom for stuffing. Lightly stuff head and top two-thirds of body with fiberfill; add doll pellets to bottom third of body and baste opening closed.

5. Stitch arms and legs together in pairs, leaving openings for stuffing where indicated. Stuff with fiberfill. Stitch openings closed by hand; stitch limbs to body where indicated.

6. Referring to photo throughout, hand-stitch muzzle to bear's face using white thread and blanket stitch. Paint black circles for eyes and paint nose with light brown; let dry. Add white highlights to eyes using toothpick and complete mouth and make heart on body front with deep red; let dry.

7. Tie ribbon in a bow around bear's neck. Tuck red fabric into pocket, and tuck in teddy bear.

Rolled Paper Coin Holder

Dad's desktop change spilling all over the place? Keep his bureau neat with this clever container for that loose change that seems to pile up so quickly. You can select the paper so it matches his bedroom decor!

Design by Helen L. Rafson

Materials

- Tuna can, thoroughly washed, dried and label removed
- No. 2 pencil
- Wrapping paper
- Tacky craft glue
- Felt for bottom (optional)

Instructions

1. From wrapping paper, cut 34 (1½" x 3") strips.

2. Lay short end of paper strip over pencil; apply a bit of glue to paper. Wrap paper around pencil, securing end with more glue. Carefully slip rolled paper off pencil; let dry. Repeat with remaining paper strips.

3. Glue seam sides of paper rolls around side of tuna can, covering can completely. Set aside to dry.

4. If desired, cut a circle of felt to fit bottom of can and glue in place.

Baby Face Jars & Gift Bags

The cutest little baby faces adorn these super-easy, super-quick projects. The little candy jars make perfect favors for guests at the baby shower, and gift bags adorned with a larger version of the faces are more fun than those pricey ready-made bags.

Design by Helen L. Rafson

Materials

Candy Jar

- Small jelly jar from Provo Crafts
- 15" piece pink or blue ¼"-wide satin ribbon
- 7½" white eyelet lace

Gift Bag

- 9¼" x 7⅞" white paper gift bag with handles
- 5⅜" x 7¼" pink or blue print fabric
- Aleene's Fusible Web by Duncan Enterprises
- 27" piece pink or blue medium or baby-size rickrack
- 1 yard white eyelet lace
- Pink or blue satin ribbon:
  6¾" piece ¼"-wide
  19½" piece 1"-wide
- 2 (⁷⁄₁₆"-diameter) white or pearl flat buttons
- Iron

All Projects

- White craft foam
- Black fine-tip permanent marking pen
- Pink cosmetic blusher
- Cotton-tip swab
- Paintbrush
- Black acrylic paint
- Curly doll hair from Darice Inc.:
  10mm lemon for girl
  13mm auburn brown for boy
- Aleene's Thick Tacky Glue by Duncan Enterprises
- Seam sealant

Project Notes

Refer to photo throughout for placement.

Instructions

Candy Jar

1. Referring to pattern for small baby face, cut one face from white craft foam.

2. Using fine-tip marking pen, add dashed line around edge of face; draw mouth. Apply cosmetic blusher to cheeks with cotton-tip swab.

3. Dip end of paintbrush into black paint and dot on eyes; let dry. Carefully add eyelashes and eyebrows with fine-tip marking pen.

4. Glue wisp of hair to top of head. Let dry.

5. Cut ¼"-wide ribbon into one 8¼" piece and one 6¾" piece. Tie shorter piece in a bow, trimming ends at an angle. Apply seam sealant to cut ends; let dry. Glue pink bow to base of hair for girl; glue blue bow to chin for boy.

6. Glue eyelet around outside edge of jar lid; let dry. Glue remaining ribbon over eyelet. Glue face to top of jar lid.

7. Fill jar with candies or mints.

Gift Bag

1. Referring to pattern for large baby face, cut face from white craft foam. Repeat steps 2–4 from instructions for candy jar.

2. Following manufacturer's instructions, fuse webbing to back of fabric; fuse fabric to front of bag. Glue on rickrack border to cover fabric edges; let dry.

3. Cut a 2¾" piece of eyelet for boy or a 3¼" piece for girl; glue to fabric for collar as shown. Glue on face; let dry.

4. Tie ¼"-wide ribbon into a bow, trimming ends at an angle. Apply seam sealant to cut ends; let dry. Glue pink bow to base of hair for girl; glue blue bow to collar below chin for boy. Glue buttons below collar.

5. Glue remaining eyelet lace around inside edge of bag opening; let dry. Tie 1"-wide ribbon in a bow around bag handle; trim ends in a V-shape and apply seam sealant; let dry.

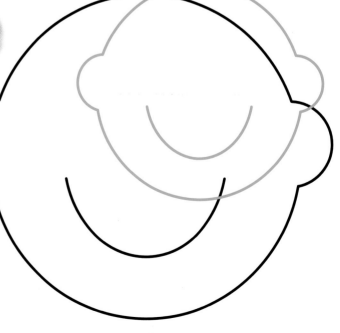

Summer Fun Baby Bibs

With just a wee bit of effort, scraps from your stash of sewing leftovers become a precious pair of bibs—a charming gift, a sure-fire seller at your next bazaar! Use a simple, inexpensive purchased bib as the base, or whip one up using a favorite pattern.

Designs by Helen L. Rafson

Materials

- 2 turquoise purchased or home-sewn baby bibs
- Solid-color fabric scraps: red, green, yellow, white, turquoise and purple
- Rickrack:
  Blue medium
  Metallic silver and red baby-size
- 3" piece of ⅜"-wide grosgrain ribbon: red, green and yellow
- Iron-on fusible webbing
- Iron
- Seam sealant
- Matching sewing threads
- White ⅝" button
- Black fine-point permanent marking pen
- Hand-sewing needle
- Sewing machine with zigzag stitch

Instructions

1. Pre-shrink all fabrics. Following manufacturer's instructions, apply fusible web to wrong side of fabrics. Referring to patterns (below and on page 160), cut sections for fish, kite and cloud from fused fabrics.

2. Treat ends of rickrack with seam sealant. Referring to photo, lay out blue rickrack waves on fish bib and sew in place with matching thread; lay out silver rickrack fishhook and sew in place with white thread.

3. Arrange fish sections on bib and fuse in place; machine-appliqué around each piece using matching thread. Hand-stitch white button to bib for fish's eye; add pupil with black fine-point marking pen.

4. Lay out kite sections and cloud on kite bib; fuse in place. Machine-appliqué around all kite sections with red, and around cloud with white. Arrange red rickrack for kite string; sew in place with red thread.

5. Tie knots in centers of ribbon pieces; trim ribbon ends to 1" and apply seam sealant to cut edges. Tack to kite string using sewing needle and matching threads.

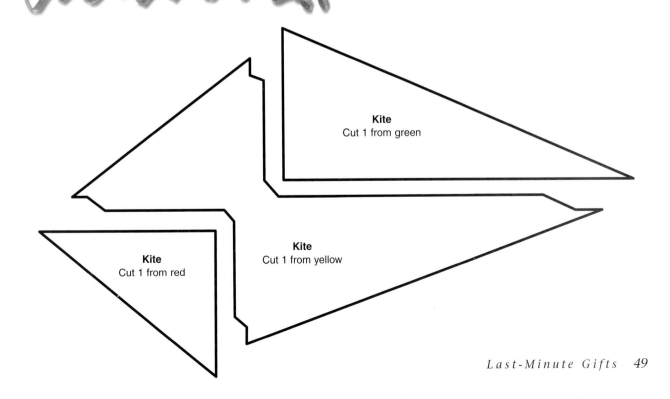

Kite
Cut 1 from green

Kite
Cut 1 from yellow

Kite
Cut 1 from red

Chilly Chums Picture Frame

Celebrate winter's special delights with this easy-to-paint frame crafted from a ready-made picture frame and "rusty" craft tin.

Design by Delores F. Ruzicka

Materials

- 8" x 10" papier-mâché picture frame with rusty tin corners by D&CC
- 8" square Rust It thin tin by Tolin' Station
- Scissors or tin snips
- Americana acrylic paints from DecoArt:
  Pumpkin #DA13
  Burgundy wine #DA22
  Blueberry #DA37
  Forest green #DA50

Lamp (ebony) black #DA67
Coral rose #DA103
Light buttermilk #DA164

- American Painter paintbrushes from Loew-Cornell:
  Series #2550 ½" wash brush
  Series #4000 #1
- Old toothbrush or stiff brush for spattering
- Crafter's Pick Ultimate Tacky Glue from API
- Matte-finish spray sealer

Project Notes

Let paint dry before applying overlaying or adjacent colors.

Refer to photo throughout.

Instructions

1. Using ½" wash brush and blueberry paint, paint papier-mâché portions of picture frame.

2. Referring to patterns (below), cut snowmen, trees and snowdrifts from tin.

3. Thin a small amount of light buttermilk with a little water. Using ½" wash brush, paint snowmen and snowdrifts with thinned paint; tin should show through

paint to give your project an antiqued appearance.

4. Using #1 brush, paint snowmen's noses with pumpkin, cheeks with coral rose and scarves with burgundy wine. Use black for eyes, mouths, buttons and detail lines.

5. Thin a small amount of forest green with a little water. Using ½" wash brush, paint trees with thinned paint. When green paint is dry, add detail lines with black and #1 brush; dab on undiluted light buttermilk to give the effect of snow on the branches.

6. Glue tin pieces to picture frame as shown. Spatter entire frame lightly with undiluted light buttermilk; dot on light buttermilk eye highlights. Spray frame with matte sealer.

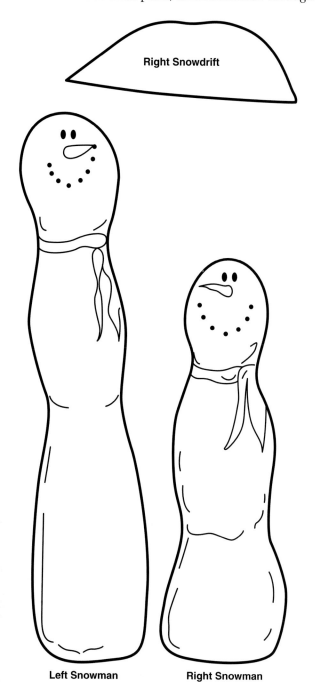

Left Snowman   **Right Snowman**

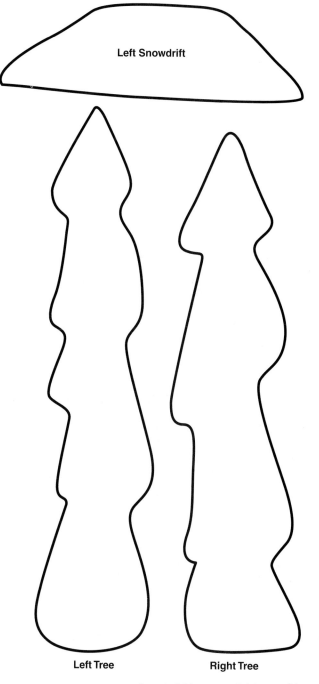

Left Tree   **Right Tree**

Gone Fishin' Gift Box

Do you know someone whose favorite vacation location is a bass boat in any body of water? Is someone storing worms in your refrigerator? This great project stands alone nicely as a lovely accent piece, but it also makes the perfect gift box for some new lures or a new reel.

Design by Rochelle Norris

Materials

- 7¾"-diameter round papier-mâché box with lid
- Ceramcoat acrylic paints from Delta Technical Coatings Inc.:
  Sandstone #2402
  Butter cream #2523
  Pine green #2526
- Paintbrush
- Spattering brush
- Scrapbook pages from Provo Craft:
  1 sheet Nature's Pastime
  2 sheets Tied Flies by The Paper Patch
- Vinyl-to-vinyl wallpaper paste
- Pens from Sakura of America:
  .03 Pigma black marking pen
  Identi Pen black marking pen

Project Notes

Let paint dry before applying overlaying or adjacent colors.

Refer to photo throughout.

Instructions

1. Cut Tied Flies pages to fit around sides of box, matching prints carefully along edges.

2. Paint lid top and sides with butter cream paint. Shade bottom edge of lid rim and outside edge of lid top with sandstone. Speckle lightly with pine green.

3. Cut fishing creel, oar and net from Nature's Pastime paper. Paste to center of lid with wallpaper paste. Allow box to dry for several hours.

4. Using marking pens, outline lid top and rim, and write "Gone Fishin'" on lid and "I was a wishin' I was a fishin'" and "Gone Fishin'" around rim, adding dots to ends of lines in letters with broad end of Identi Pen.

Catch of the Day Frame

Preserve a picture of the one that didn't get away in this fun frame!

Design by Debbie Rines

Materials
- Small frame #3591 from Walnut Hollow
- 3 wooden fish #U10684 from Lara's Crafts
- 5 brass screw eyes #U10078 from Lara's Crafts
- 3 small fishing swivels
- 2 small fly hooks
- 12" brass chain
- 16" monofilament fishing line or heavy clear thread
- Wooden chopstick
- ½" flat button
- Aleene's wood-finishing products by Duncan Enterprises:
  Oak wood stain #AW 105
  Clear wood stain #AW 101
  Satin varnish #EN 102
- Aleene's Premium Coat acrylic paints by Duncan Enterprises:
  Light orange #OC 113
  Deep sage #OC 134
  True grey #OC 175
  Black #OC 176
  Silver #OC 303
- Aleene's Thick Designer Tacky Glue by Duncan Enterprises
- Toothpick
- Paintbrushes:
  #10 flat
  #10/0 liner
  ¾" flat
  Spattering brush
- Sponge applicator
- Paper towels
- Wire cutters
- Needle-nose pliers
- Craft knife

Project Notes

Let all stain, paint and varnish dry before applying

overlaying or adjacent colors or proceeding with assembly.

Staining & Painting

1. Mix 2 parts oak stain with 1 part clear stain for a light, golden oak tone (use undiluted oak stain if you prefer a deeper oak color). Apply this mixture to frame, a small area at a time, and wipe off excess with paper towel.

2. Cut 5¾" section from broad end of chopstick; stain with diluted mixture, wiping off all excess stain.

3. Using #10 flat brush through step 4, double-load with light orange and silver. Apply along bottom half of fish (silver on bottom of fish, light orange in center), from nose to tail, to make stripes. Continue around edges and paint both sides of fish.

4. Double-load brush with light orange and deep sage. Apply along top half of fish, from nose to tail (deep sage on top, light orange in center), and continue around edges to paint both sides of fish.

5. Using damp #10/0 liner brush, brush-mix small amounts of true grey and black and paint short, irregular lines on tail. Lightly tap tip of brush to make irregular spots on fish. Add small black dot for eye.

6. Using dry #10 flat brush, dry-brush black onto the chopstick. Paint inside edge of frame black. Let dry.

7. Using spattering brush or old toothbrush, spatter frame with black.

8. Using ¾" flat brush, apply satin varnish to frame, fish and chopstick.

Assembly

1. Attach screw eye to mouth of each fish; screw two more into top edge of frame, each about 1" from edge of frame.

2. Using needle-nose pliers, open last link of chain; attach to screw eye on right side of frame. Close link. Attach to left screw eye in same manner, leaving enough chain between screw eyes to hang picture. Let remaining chain hang down front on left side of frame. Hook a swivel in each screw eye in fish and attach to chain. Glue fish in place.

Continued on page 160

Wearable Crafts

Craft, then wear each of these
fun and creative projects! Your
friends will admire your skill,
and the many eye-catching
garments and accessories
added to your wardrobe!

Rag Doll Pin

*Let this sweet little someone keep you company to remind you that life is full of whimsy —
and a delightful surprise might be just around the bend!*

Design by Helen Rafson

Materials

- 5" circle light pink fabric
- Tiny scrap of lightweight red fabric
- 2 (6mm) black half-round balls from Westrim Trimming Corp.
- Polyester fiberfill
- 2⅝" piece ⅞"-wide white eyelet lace
- Red acrylic yarn
- Seam sealant
- Aleene's fusible web by Duncan Enterprises
- Aleene's Tacky Glue by Duncan Enterprises
- Coordinating sewing thread
- Hand-sewing needle
- Black fine-line permanent marking pen
- Powdered cosmetic blusher
- Cotton-tip swab
- Iron
- 1" pin back

Project Note

Refer to photo throughout.

Instructions

1. Following manufacturer's instructions, fuse web to back of red fabric. Referring to pattern above, cut one nose triangle from fused fabric.

2. Using fine-line pen, draw mouth onto pink fabric circle; peel backing from nose and fuse to face. Glue half-balls in place for eyes and add eyebrows with marking pen.

3. Sew a gathering stitch around fabric circle ¼" from edge; pull thread ends to gather slightly. Place ball of fiberfill in center of circle and pull gathering thread tight; knot off and clip ends.

4. Using cotton swab, apply blusher to cheeks.

5. Cut two strands of yarn each 3¼" long; holding strands together, tie knot in center and clip yarn to ¾" long on both sides of knot. Repeat to make enough hair to cover head. Applying glue to knots only, glue

individual yarn bunches to head in two or three rows. Let glue dry; trim hair evenly.

6. Apply seam sealant to ends of eyelet. Glue under face for collar. Glue or stitch pin back to wrong side of pin.

Rag Doll Pin

Kitty Cats Vest

Talk about easy! Cut cat shapes from a variety of soft "flocked" fabrics and fuse them to a ready-made denim vest for a quick wearable that's the perfect addition to all your country-casual fashions!

Design by Deborah Brooks

Materials

- Denim vest from Innovo Inc.
- Fusible web
- Fabrics from J & J Flock Products Inc.:
  ¼ yard cashmere single-face fine dernier rayon
  ¼ yard mocha double-face fine dernier rayon
  ¼ yard doeskin nylon
  ¼ yard mink acrylic
- Iron

Project Notes

Patterns are given in a single size. Use a photocopier with enlarging capabilities to make cats and paw prints of different sizes as desired to decorate your vest.

Refer to photo throughout.

Instructions

1. Prewash vest without using fabric softener; dry. Press.

2. Photocopy patterns (page 161) in desired sizes, reversing a few as desired; plan their placement on vest front and back.

3. Following manufacturer's instructions, iron fusible web onto wrong side of fabrics. Trace cats and paw prints onto paper backing; cut out.

4. Fuse cats and paw prints to vest. ●

Stars & Cats T-Shirt

If a cat is the star of your household, don't deny it … don't try to hide it … celebrate it! Whip up this colorful T-shirt—and then whip open that tuna can to give your "star" a special treat!

Design by Barbara A. Woolley

Materials

- White T-shirt
- ⅛ yard of each of seven coordinating star-patterned fabrics
- 1 yard Steam-a-Seam 2 fusible web from The Warm Company
- T-shirt painting board
- Iron

Project Note

Refer to photo throughout for placement.

Instructions

1. Wash and dry T-shirt without using fabric softener; press as needed to remove wrinkles. Place T-shirt over painting board and pin or hold with rubber bands as needed to make shirt lie smooth.

2. Following manufacturer's instructions, fuse web to back of fabrics. Referring to patterns (pages 161 and 162), cut eight fish, reversing four, from one of the prints. Cut two M's (one will be turned upside down for W), one E and one O from a second print for "MEOW." From each of remaining five print fabrics, cut two cats, reversing one.

3. Position "MEOW," four fish and six cats on shirt front as shown. Following manufacturer's instructions, fuse cats, fish and "MEOW" to shirt. Fuse remaining cats and fish to back of shirt. ●

Blooming Roses Sweatshirt

Enjoy bountiful blooming roses anytime when you wear this glittering sweatshirt.
The painting technique uses a bunch of celery as a brush!

Design by Doxie Keller

Materials

- Burgundy sweatshirt
- Plastic-coated freezer paper
- Shirt-painting board
- ¾" masking tape
- 1 bunch celery
- So-Soft acrylic fabric paints from DecoArt:
  White #DSS1
  Raspberry pink #DSS8
  Cranberry wine #DSS29
- Shimmering Pearls fabric paints from DecoArt:
  Lime #DSP9
  Teal #DSP11
- Gold Glitter #DD303 So-Soft Dimensional fabric paint from DecoArt
- ¾" white nylon paintbrush #798 from Loew-Cornell
- Miracle Sponge or small silk sponge
- Iron

Project Note

Refer to photo throughout.

Instructions

1. Launder shirt without using fabric softener; dry. Turn shirt wrong side out. Setting your iron for cotton, iron freezer paper, coated side down, onto wrong side of sweatshirt around neckline. This stabilizes fabric and keeps paint from seeping through. Turn shirt right side out and put over shirt-painting board.

2. Place masking tape strip down center of shirt, extending 6½" down from neckline ribbing. Place additional masking-tape strips 3" to left and right of center strip, extending strips 7" down from shoulder seams. Place a final pair of strips 3" further to the outside extending 3½" down from shoulder seam.

3. Place tape at shoulder seam to block paint and in a diagonal line along bottom of taped strips. Run a second strip from other side so tapes meet at center front. Dip sponge into raspberry and white paints and sponge areas between tape strips. Let paint dry 15–30 minutes.

4. Cut straight through bunch of celery 4" from stem; cut surface must be flat to print.

5. Brush or sponge a heavy load of paint onto cut surface of celery, applying cranberry in center, raspberry toward outside and white along edges. Stamp paint-coated celery on shirt and twist a quarter-turn. Repeat to make additional roses as desired. Let paint dry for 15–30 minutes.

6. Outline and accent roses with Gold Glitter dimensional paint.

7. Fill paintbrush with lime paint and add some teal on left side of brush. Making just one or two strokes per leaf, add leaves to roses. Let dry 15–30 minutes; outline and add veins with Gold Glitter dimensional paint.

8. Allow paints to cure for 72 hours; no heat-setting is required. For best results, launder by hand and hang on a plastic or wooden hanger to dry. After 3 weeks, the shirt can be dried in the dryer. Gold paint will feel tacky, but it can be worn after 24 hours drying time. ●

Fast & Fancy Socks

Here's a great project to share with your children! In no time at all, you can transform basic bargain-basement socks into one-of-a-kind, "boutique-style" originals!

Designs by Joan Fee

Buttoned-Up Socks

Materials

- Aleene's Jewel-It Glue by Duncan Enterprises
- White cuffed ankle socks
- Flat buttons in assorted sizes and colors
- Plastic-wrapped cardboard to fit inside sock

Instructions

1. Insert plastic-wrapped cardboard into sock so glue will not bleed through to other side of sock.

2. Place a dot of glue on cuff; position button over glue and press so glue comes up through holes. Continue, adding additional buttons as desired.

3. Let socks "cure" for one week before laundering. To launder, turn socks so buttons are on inside.

Blooming Daisy Socks

Materials

- Silk daisies
- Trouser socks
- Aleene's Paper Napkin Appliqué Glue by Duncan Enterprises
- Dimensional fabric paints: black and green
- 2 jars (to slightly stretch socks)
- ½" flat paintbrush
- Iron

Project Note

Refer to photo throughout.

Instructions

1. Separate layers of silk daisies; iron with low heat to flatten them.

2. Insert jars in sock openings to stretch socks slightly and smoothly.

3. With paintbrush, apply glue where daisy will be placed. Position daisy over glued area; press flat with fingers. Brush additional glue over daisy and onto sock slightly beyond edges of petals. Add more daisies as desired, using the same method.

4. Use black paint to add dots to centers of daisies. With green paint, draw simple leaves as desired.

5. Let socks "cure" for one week before laundering. To launder, turn socks so daisies are on inside. ●

Valentine Pin

Alphabet beads, wooden heart cutouts and a few paints quickly meld to make a sweet valentine remembrance. Give it a try, and you'll see how simple it is to adapt the procedure for other designs, messages and color choices. It's a super tuck-in for valentine cards, too.

Design by Judy Atwell

Materials

- 2 (1½"-wide) wooden heart cutouts
- 4 tiny lettered glass beads: L, O, V and E
- Ceramcoat acrylic paints from Delta Technical Coatings Inc.:
  Napthol crimson #2408
  White #2505
  Black #2506
  14K gold #2604
- Small round sable paintbrush
- Gold glitter dimensional writer
- Aerosol acrylic spray
- Super Strength all-purpose adhesive from 3M
- 1½" pin back
- Straight pin

Project Notes

Allow all paints and glues to dry thoroughly between applications.

Refer to photo throughout. The paint choices and designs shown are but one option. Experiment with different colors and designs. Don't worry about perfectly forming every line or dot; have fun painting, and your finished pin will reflect it!

Instructions

1. Paint front and edges of one heart gold and the other white.

2. Paint a narrow black line around top of white heart and a narrow white line around top of gold heart. With the tip of the paintbrush, paint napthol crimson dots atop both lines.

3. Applying paint only with the side of the brush, paint a very narrow crimson line around top edge of white heart. Using same technique, apply black to top edge of gold heart. Add a row of black dots around gold heart inside red dots. Add a second row of dots to white heart using gold glitter writer.

4. Glue gold heart atop white heart, overlapping them as shown.

5. Line up beads to spell "LOVE" on a straight pin. While they are still on the pin, glue them to the gold heart. Once glue has set for a few minutes, slide out pin.

6. Spray front of hearts with acrylic spray. Glue pin back to back of hearts. ●

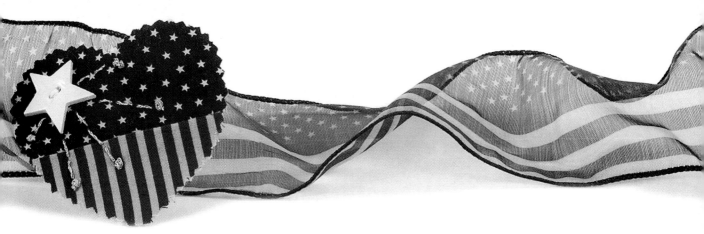

Americana Lapel Pin

Wear your patriotic pride on your lapel this Fourth of July or any time!
This simple fabric pin sews up in a flash and looks great with any casual fashions.

Design by Leslie Hartsock

Materials

- 2" x 4" piece blue fabric with white stars
- 2" x 4" red/cream striped fabric
- 4" square coordinating fabric for backing
- 4" square Pellon fusible fleece
- 2 (4") squares Pellon Heavy-Duty Wonder-Under fusible web
- White ceramic star button #86181 from Mill Hill
- DMC gold metallic embroidery floss
- White sewing thread
- Needle
- 1" pin back
- Iron
- Pinking shears
- Sewing machine (optional)
- Hot-glue gun (optional)

Project Note

Refer to photo throughout.

Instructions

1. Stitch fabric pieces together, wrong sides facing, along one long edge using ¼" seam allowance. Iron, pressing seam open.

2. Following manufacturer's instructions, fuse web to wrong side of seamed fabric and to wrong side of backing fabric. Remove paper; sandwich fleece between fused fabrics and press to secure layers.

3. Referring to pattern, trace heart onto backing fabric. Cut out with pinking shears.

4. Using white thread, sew ceramic star to top left of heart. Using metallic gold floss, sew rows of running stitches for "rays" extending from star; end each ray in a French knot.

5. Sew or glue pin back in place. ●

Americana Lapel Pin

All-Star Dad Sweatshirt

Make this colorful tribute for your favorite father figure! It's quick and easy, thanks to simple patterns and fusible interfacing. Why not select a sweatshirt and fabric colors to mimic his favorite team's colors?

Design by Helen Rafson

Materials

- Sweatshirt
- 6" x 8" piece of each of three print fabrics: blue, green and red
- Small piece of gold fabric
- Sewing threads: gold and coordinating color to match fabrics
- Aleene's fusible web by Duncan Enterprises
- Fabric stabilizer
- Water-soluble marking pen (optional)
- Sewing machine with zigzag stitch
- Iron

Project Note

Refer to photo throughout.

Instructions

1. Launder sweatshirt and fabrics without using fabric softener; let dry and press as needed.

2. Fold sweatshirt in half matching shoulder and side seams. Mark center line with pins, basting thread or water-soluble marker.

3. Following manufacturer's instructions, fuse web to backs of fabrics. Referring to patterns (page 163), trace one D onto paper backing on blue print fabric and one onto backing on green; trace one A onto backing on red fabric and one star onto backing on gold fabric; cut out.

4. Position letters on front of sweatshirt, centering them carefully. Peel paper backing from letters and fuse to shirt. Peel backing from star and fuse to A.

5. Pin stabilizer smoothly to wrong side of shirt behind letters. Thread sewing machine with gold thread to match star; machine-appliqué around star. Thread machine with second thread color and machine-appliqué around each letter.

6. Carefully trim stabilizer from back of shirt. ●

Lacy White Shorts Set

Transform the simplest white boxer shorts and T-shirt into a feminine, lacy delight.

Design by Sandy Dye

Materials

- White cotton boxer shorts
- White V-neck cotton T-shirt
- 4 yards (2") white Cluny lace
- 1½" white lace heart motif
- Double-face white satin ribbon:
  4 yards (⅛")
  1½ yards (¼")
  1¾ yards (1½")
- ¾" elastic measuring twice your hip measurement plus 2"
- ½" crystal heart cabochon
- Washable craft cement
- Sewing machine or hand-sewing needle
- White sewing thread

Project Notes

Amounts of Cluny lace and ribbon may vary with size of garments used.

Refer to photo throughout.

Instructions

1. Measure and cut lace to fit around bottom of each leg, adding ½" for turning under ends. Weave ¼"-wide ribbon through openings in top of lace. Pin lace around leg hems; stitch through top of lace.

2. Measure and cut lace to fit around neckline of T-shirt; weave ⅛"-wide ribbon through openings in top of lace. Pin woven lace around neckline beginning at bottom of V. Stitch along top of lace, turning under ends. Stitch through lace a second time, stitching just below ⅛"-wide ribbon. Sew lace heart motif at bottom of V over ends.

3. Finger-press a crease on sleeve from shoulder down. Measure and cut two pieces of lace ¼" longer than crease in sleeve. Weave ⅛"-wide ribbon through each piece, leaving an extra 9" of ribbon. Referring to Fig. 1, stitch both pieces of lace, flat edges facing, down crease of sleeve, turning lace edges under at top and bottom of sleeve. Turn under ribbon edges at bottom of sleeve and stitch in place, leaving excess ribbon ends free at shoulder. Stitch through lace a second time, stitching

just on other side of ribbon. Gently pull ribbon ends at shoulder to gather sleeve a bit; tie in a bow and trim ribbon ends as desired.

4. Repeat step 3 for second sleeve.

5. Measure 7½" up from shirt hem all around; lay 1½"-wide ribbon in place, matching bottom edge of ribbon to mark. Turning under ends, stitch ribbon in place on bottom edge. Smooth ribbon flat; stitch in place along top edge. Stitch a third seam down center of ribbon.

6. Cut two pieces of elastic 1" larger than your hip measurement. Thread one piece through each of the two channels stitched in the 1½"-wide ribbon; secure elastic and close ribbon openings.

7. Tie a bow from remaining 1½"-wide ribbon; stitch to ribbon on shirt, placing it off-center. Gather 8" Cluny lace into a pouf and sew to center of bow; glue cabochon to center of pouf. ●

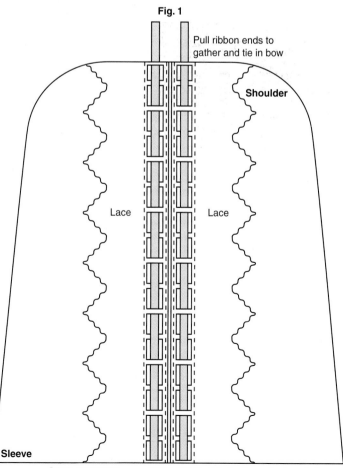

Fig. 1

Pull ribbon ends to gather and tie in bow

Shoulder

Lace   Lace

Sleeve

Stitch down lace where indicated

Stitch ribbon ends in place at edge of sleeve

Gum-Ball Vest

Novelty fabrics are a real boon to crafters who love quick and easy projects. This design incorporates brightly colored "smiley faces" cut from fabric and applied quickly and easily to a ready-made denim vest. Your child will love it!

Design by Deborah Brooks

Materials

- Child's denim vest from Innovo Inc.
- ½ yard Happy Face fabric from The Cranston Collection
- 4" x 2½" piece red felt
- Fusible web
- Tulip slick dimensional paints from Duncan Enterprises:
  White #65000
  Slate gray #65165
- Iron
- Cardboard

Project Note

Refer to photo throughout.

Instructions

1. Prewash vest and Happy Face fabric without using fabric softener; dry. Press.

2. Following manufacturer's instructions, apply fusible web to back of red felt and Happy Face fabric.

3. Referring to pattern (page 164, cut base of gum-ball machine from red felt. Cut smiling faces from fabric. Referring to pattern, cut dispenser opening for gum-ball machine from black background of fabric.

4. Fuse base to center back of vest 2" from bottom edge; fuse black opening to base. Fuse smiling "gum balls" to front and back of vest, positioning a few so that they will be "inside" the gum-ball machine.

5. Trace round "glass dispenser" onto cardboard; cut out. Position cardboard pattern over red felt base and trace around it with white 3D paint; add accent lines and "5¢" as shown. Outline base with slate gray paint. Let vest lay flat until paint is completely dry. ●

Moo-Cows Shorts Set

Beautiful bovines are showing up everywhere! If you're one of the many who can't get enough of cows, enhance your collection with this quick and easy knit shirt-and-shorts set. The results are udderly delightful!

Design by Barbara A. Woolley

Materials

- White knit baseball-style shirt with black stripes or shirt of your choice
- Black knit shorts or shorts of your choice
- ⅛ yard of four different black-and-white print fabrics
- 1 yard Steam-a-Seam 2 fusible web from The Warm Company
- 1 piece washable pink felt
- Pink satin ribbon:
  2 yards (⅛")
  1½ yards (¼")
- Fabric glue
- Black buttons for shirt
- 10 tiny cow bells
- Pink sewing thread
- Hand-sewing needle
- Iron

Project Note

Refer to photo throughout.

Instructions

1. Wash and dry shirt and shorts without using fabric softener; press as needed to remove wrinkles.

2. Following manufacturer's instructions, fuse web to back of fabrics and felt. Referring to patterns (page 164), cut 10 cows from assorted patterns, reversing five; from pink felt, cut 10 udders, reversing five, plus four M's and eight O's.

3. Lay out cows and "MOO's" on shirt and shorts. One cow is positioned at bottom of one leg; eight cows and three "MOO's" are arranged on front of shirt; remaining cow and "MOO" are positioned on back of shirt, approximately at left shoulder blade.

4. When arrangement pleases you, cut a piece of ⅛"-wide pink ribbon to reach each cow on shirt from shoulder seam or neckline so cows will appear to "hang" from ends of ribbons. Glue ribbons to shirt.

5. Following manufacturer's instructions, fuse cows, udders and "MOO's" to shirt, covering ribbon ends.

Fuse remaining cow and udder to shorts.

6. Stitch cow bell to neck of each cow.

7. Cut ¼"-wide ribbon into 10 equal pieces; tie each in a bow and glue one to top of each cow.

8. Remove shirt's original buttons. Sew black buttons to shirt with pink thread. ●

Bazaar Bestsellers

Craft a crop of money-making winners for your next bazaar or craft sale with this collection of more than a dozen fun and easy-to-make projects!

Straw Hat Garden Collection

*Imagine the squeals of delight when your mother-daughter banquet guests
sit down to tables decorated with these cute little favors and quickie place cards!
They work up so quickly, you can turn out a whole basketful in no time!*

Designs by Angie Wilhite

Materials

Each Favor

- 1¾"-diameter terra-cotta flower pot
- 2½"-diameter straw hat
- 3 (½") pink ribbon rosettes from Wrights
- 8" piece of ⅛"-wide green satin ribbon
- 2 (7mm) round black movable eyes
- Air-soluble pen
- Fine-line black permanent marking pen
- Aleene's Ultimate glue gun and jewelry glue sticks by Duncan Enterprises

Garden Lady Favor

Project Note

Refer to photo (page 68) throughout.

Instructions

1. Cut ribbon into two 3" pieces and one 2" piece. Glue a ribbon rosette to one end of each of the longer pieces; glue ribbon ends next to each other inside rim of flower pot; this becomes the front of flower pot.

2. Fold 2" piece of ribbon into a figure eight with ends in center; glue ribbon rosette to straw hat over ends of figure eight so green ribbon forms "leaves." Glue hat to bottom of flower pot, tilting it as shown.

3. Glue eyes to front of flower pot. Draw smile with air-soluble pen, then trace over it with black marking pen.

4. If desired, decorate the buffet table with larger versions of the garden lady made with proportionately larger flower pots, straw hats, wiggle eyes and wider ribbon.

Materials

Each Place Card

- 3"-diameter straw hat
- ½" pink ribbon rosette from Wrights
- 2" piece of ⅛"-wide green satin ribbon
- Aleene's Ultimate glue gun and jewelry glue sticks by Duncan Enterprises

Straw Hat Place Card

Project Note

Refer to photo (above) throughout.

Instructions

1. Fold ribbon into a figure eight with ends in center; glue ribbon rosette to straw hat over ends of figure eight so green ribbon forms "leaves."

2. Hang hat over corner of place card and glue as shown.

M a t e r i a l s

Each Pair

- 3 clean white crew socks (see Project Notes)
- 2 (1") wooden spools
- Polyester doll pellets
- Polyester fiberfill
- Hand-sewing needle and white thread
- Kunin Felt:
  1 sheet white #550 Rainbow Plush Felt
  2" x 3⅜" piece cadet blue #656 Rainbow Felt Classic
- Denim from cast-off jeans:
  3" x 9½" piece with stitched hem along one long side
  2 (3½") pieces cut from flat seam
- Black extra-fine-line permanent marking pen
- Speedball Painters fine-point Opaque Paint Markers: pink and royal blue
- Pink crayon
- 2 (4") straw hats

- Tulip Pearl Paint from Duncan Enterprises:
  Soft yellow #65045
  Pink #65052
  Sea mist #65067
- Americana acrylic paints from DecoArt:
  Pumpkin #DA13
  Kelly green #DA55
- Several ⅝" x ½" pieces of bright plaid fabric
- 21" (⅝"-wide) light blue ribbon
- 2 (⅜") blue buttons
- 2 (¼") pale pink ribbon rosettes
- ½" rose pink ribbon rosette
- 3 small green silk rose leaves
- 2 (2") white pompoms
- White carpet thread
- White waxed dental floss
- Magic Pro glue gun and High Performance low-temperature glue sticks from Adhesive Technologies Inc.

Farmer Bunny & His Bride

Just on their way to market to sell the roots of their labors, these sweet country bunnies are easy to make from inexpensive white socks.

Designs by Janna Britton

Project Notes

For sample projects (page 70), boys' socks in size 7–8½ were used.

Refer to photo throughout for placement.

Farmer Bunny

1. Referring to Fig. 1 (page 165), lay one sock flat and cut through both layers as shown to make one bunny.

2. Using needle and white carpet thread, gather ribbed edge of sock cuff closed to form flat area; glue spool inside sock at flat area. Pour doll pellets inside body to cover spool, then stuff remainder of bunny with fiberfill.

3. With needle and white carpet thread, gather top of bunny's head to close where indicated, leaving ear section open. Cut ear section in half to make two ears.

4. Wrap white carpet thread around bunny 2" below top of head; tighten thread to make bunny's neck and knot securely.

5. Referring to patterns (page 165), cut one set of feet and four arms, reversing two, from white plush felt. Glue arms together in pairs, flat sides of felt facing. Glue feet to bottom of bunny, plush side up, and tops of arms to shoulder area.

6. Draw eyes, nose and mouth on bunny with black extra-fine-line marking pen. Color in features with paint markers, using royal blue for eyes and pink for nose. Blush cheeks with pink crayon.

7. *Whiskers:* Knot end of dental floss leaving 1" tail; thread floss into needle and insert needle through bunny's face, going in at base of one whisker and coming out at the base of whisker on other side of face; knot off other end close to face and trim other whisker to 1" length. Repeat to add other whiskers.

8. *Overalls:* Wrap denim rectangle around body with hemmed edge at bottom and overlapping ends in back; glue in place. Define legs by stitching long lines with carpet thread 1½" up on center of denim to bottom, stitching from front to back; pull thread tightly and knot. Glue fabric patches to overalls as desired. Glue denim flat-seam pieces over shoulders

for overall straps.

9. Arrange ears so they hang to sides; glue hat to bunny's head.

10. Glue pompom tail to bottom back of Farmer Bunny.

Mrs. Bunny

1. Referring to steps 1–4 for Farmer Bunny, cut another sock to make Mrs. Bunny. To form head, gather lower ribbed edge together so she will be a bit shorter than Farmer Bunny. Repeat steps 5–7 for Farmer Bunny.

2. *Apron:* Round off two bottom corners of cadet blue felt (along one long edge) with scissors. Add decoration with pearl paints, using pink for "stitched" border and flower petals in corners; soft yellow for flower centers; sea mist for leaves; and a few additional dots of pink for "buds," if desired. Let apron dry.

3. Finger-gather top edge of apron; glue to front of body. Wrap light blue ribbon around bunny over top edge of apron and tie ends in bow in back.

4. Glue blue buttons to Mrs. Bunny above apron.

5. Decorate bottom edge of hat brim with royal blue paint marker; let dry. Glue leaves and ribbon rosettes to base of hat crown as shown; arrange Mrs. Bunny's ears as desired and glue hat to Mrs. Bunny's head with flowers in front. "Smoosh" hat down in center.

Carrot

1. Cut remaining sock as shown; roll on the diagonal to form a long, narrow cone; glue edge. Stuff carrot with doll pellets. Gather opening closed 1" from top; wrap with thread and knot to close securely.

2. Using acrylic paints, paint carrot pumpkin and carrot top kelly green; let dry.

3. With scissors, fringe carrot top in ¼"-wide strips. ▪

"To Die-t For" Fridgie Magnets

Sometimes a little nudge of encouragement is all it takes to resist that extra sweet, or encourage a healthy snack in instead of a diet-breaking alternative. That's the goal behind these colorful magnets.

Designs by Joanna Randolph Rott

Project Notes

Refer to photo throughout.

Allow all paints, ink, varnish and glue to dry thoroughly between coats and applications.

Instructions

1. Cut an octagon from each color of craft foam, using wooden octagon as a pattern and cutting foam pieces ⅛" larger all around. Set aside.

2. Paint each wooden octagon with a different color of acrylic paint, applying two coats to both sides and edges.

3. Trim photo to fit wooden shape and glue to black octagon.

4. Using black marking pen, letter remaining octagons with one of these mottos: She Who Stuffs Puffs, Taste Makes Waist, He Who Indulges Bulges, Think Thin Thin Thin, Diet Diet Diet.

5. Dip end of paintbrush handle in black paint and "stamp" black dots onto ends of letters. Using same technique, add dots of other colors to lettered octagons.

6. Brush one coat of varnish onto edges and lettered surfaces of octagons.

7. Using toothpick, apply a thin coat of glue to back of each wooden octagon. Press each onto a foam shape, aligning the edges or positioning them so points of foam and wooden pieces alternate. Let dry.

8. Using toothpick dipped in black paint, add accent dots to foam "frame" around photo octagon.

9. Press magnet onto back of each foam octagon. ■

Materials

Set of 6 Magnets

- 6 Woodsie large (1½") wooden octagons from Forster Inc.
- Small pieces of craft foam: green, yellow, blue, pink, purple, peach
- Ceramcoat acrylic paints from Delta Technical Coatings Inc.:
  Luscious lemon #2004
  Cape Cod blue #2133
  Bright red #2503
  Black #2506
  Colonial blue #2058
  Pretty pink #2088
- Ceramcoat satin varnish from Delta Technical Coatings Inc.
- Paintbrush
- Gem-Tac adhesive from Beacon Adhesives
- 6 (1¾") square or round adhesive-backed magnets from Magnetic Specialty Inc.
- Small photo of dieter (optional)
- Black fine-line permanent marking pen
- 2 round toothpicks

Beaded Memory Album

This project is especially easy because — believe it or not! — the beading is ironed on.

Design by Barbara Woolley

Materials

- Self-Stick Create-A-Binder from Pres-On Corp.
- Beads-2-Fuse kit with Steam-A-Seam 2 fusible web from The Warm Company
- Memory Album Batting from Fairfield
- 26" x 16" piece fabric with small floral pattern
- ¼ yard coordinating cord, rickrack or other trim
- 25" x 10" coordinating felt, plush felt or other non-raveling fabric
- Fabri-Tac fabric adhesive from Beacon Adhesives
- Iron
- Pinking shears (optional)
- Air-soluble marker or pencil
- Double-stick tape
- Poster board
- Screwdriver

Project Notes

Refer to photo throughout.

Beading Fabric

1. Following instructions which accompany memory album, cut fabric to proper size.

2. Cut fusible web to fit fabric to be beaded (it does not have to be a single solid piece).

3. Peel off backing to expose sticky side of fusible web. Place sticky side against right side of fabric; trace shapes you wish to bead with marker or pencil. Peel web from fabric and cut out shapes.

4. Place cut-out shapes back on fabric and remove other piece of paper backing, exposing second sticky side.

5. Following manufacturer's instructions, apply beads. Use beaded fabric to cover album.

Covering Album

1. Remove pages from album. Open album and place over wrong side of beaded fabric. Measure and cut fabric 1½" larger than album all around.

2. Place album on batting; trace edge with pen and cut out batting.

3. Cut two fabric strips 3¼" wide and same length as spine of album. Apply double-stick tape to one long edge of wrong side of each piece.

4. Slide tape side of fabric under left of metal spine using screwdriver to help push it under tight spots. Apply double-stick tape to other side of strip and stick in place. Repeat for right side of spine.

5. Center batting over wrong side of fabric. Place album, opened flat, over batting. Using double-stick tape and referring to Fig. 1 (page 165), secure fabric over all four corners.

6. Apply double-stick tape over complete bottom edge of album (Fig. 2). At end of metal spine, fold raw edge of fabric under ¼" and use screwdriver to help slide folded edge under spine.

7. Repeat step 6 on top edge. Check often to make sure fabric is smooth on front. Do the same on side edges, making sure top and bottom folds and side folds meet perfectly at corners to form a mitered corner.

8. Cut trim in half; glue pieces to inside of album cover around top and bottom of metal spine to cover seam between spine and cover; cut off excess trim.

9. Using pinking shears if desired, cut two pieces of felt

Continued on page 165

Elegant Treasure Pouches

Today's gift presentations include decorative sacks, bags and containers of all kinds, adding interest and an air of mystery to every present! It's so easy to adapt the colors and sizes of these pouches to fit every occasion and gift!

Designs by Nancy Marshall

Materials

Both Treasure Pouches

- 8" circles of Rainbow Felt Classic from Kunin Felt:
  Antique gold #353
  Orchid #758
- ⅛"-wide grosgrain ribbon: ¾ yard each green and metallic gold
- ⅛" round hole punch
- Glittery dimensional fabric paints: green, red and gold
- Beads from The Beadery:
  2 red pony beads
  2 (10mm) gold metallic melon beads
- Tapestry needle (optional)

Instructions

1. Around the edge of each felt circle, ½" from edge, punch 30 holes, evenly spaced about ¾" apart. Use a compass to help plot the positions of holes, if desired.

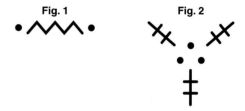

2. Referring to Fig. 1, paint design randomly over surface of orchid felt using glittery gold paint. Repeat with Fig. 2 and antique gold felt, using glittery red for dotted "holly berries" and glittery green for "leaves." Let painted circles dry flat for one day.

3. Beginning with ribbon ends to painted side of felt, and keeping ribbon flat, weave gold metallic ribbon through holes in orchid felt, using needle as desired. Slide gold bead onto each end of ribbon and knot to hold beads in place. Repeat with green ribbon, red pony beads and antique gold felt.

4. Pull ribbon ends to gather circle into a pouch and tie in a bow.

"Gone Fishing" Pillow

Only the most basic sewing skills are needed to whip up this simple, colorful felt pillow.
It makes a soft, cuddly spot to rest your head while you dream about "the one that got away."

Design by Barbara Woolley

Materials

- 12" square pillow form
- ½ yard gray fleece fabric
- 1½ yards washable forest green fringe trim
- 1 square gold craft felt
- Black dimensional fabric paint
- 6 (6") squares Fabric A
- 6 (6") squares Fabric B (see Project Notes)
- 4 (1") plastic red-and-white fishing bobbers
- Steam-a-Seam 2 double-sided iron-on fusible web from The Warm Company
- Sewing machine (optional)
- Hand-sewing needle
- Gray sewing thread
- Red button or carpet thread
- Iron

Project Notes

Each of the Fabric B squares should coordinate with one of the Fabric A squares.

Refer to photo throughout.

Instructions

1. Following manufacturer's instructions, fuse web to backs of gold felt, fabric A and fabric B squares.

2. Referring to patterns (page 166), cut letters from gold felt, cutting two each I's, N's and G's and one of each remaining letter. Cut six fish bodies from Fabric A squares, reversing a few of the fish as desired. Cut fins and heads for each fish from coordinating Fabric B squares, reversing fins and heads to match bodies.

3. Cut two 13" squares gray fleece. With right sides facing, sandwich green fringe trim between edges of fleece with fringe facing inward; pin as needed to hold in place. Stitch pillow halves and fringe together using ½"–¾" seam allowance and leaving a 5" opening for turning and stuffing. Clip corners as needed; turn pillow cover right side out.

4. Following manufacturer's instructions, peel paper backing from fabric pieces and fuse letters and fish to pillow.

5. With black paint, add fish eyes, "stringer" and imitation stitches on fish and letters.

6. Stuff pillow form into cover; stitch opening closed. Sew bobber to each corner with red thread. ▪

Chenille Chickens

*Chickens are one of today's hottest home-decor accents! You can quickly work
up a roost full using chenille fabric, felt scraps, and a couple of wooden dowels.
The finished fowl will be happy to peck along your hearth or tabletop.*

Design by Barbara Woolley

Materials

Each Chicken

- ½ yard white chenille fabric
- 4" square red felt
- 3" square orange felt
- 6" square of ¾"-thick wood stock
- 2 (⅜"-diameter) wooden dowels, 5"–8" long (depending on how tall you want finished chickens to be)
- 2 (½") flat buttons for eyes
- 2 (1") flat buttons for wings
- Polyester fiberfill
- Sewing machine (optional)
- Hand-sewing needle
- Long doll needle
- Matching thread
- Orange acrylic paint
- Paintbrush
- Sandpaper
- Scroll saw
- Drill with ⅜" bit
- Hot-glue gun
- Corrugated cardboard (optional)
- Dry beans or doll pellets (optional)

Project Notes

Allow paints and finishes to dry thoroughly between coats.

Refer to photo throughout.

Instructions

1. Referring to patterns (pages 167 and 168), cut two feet from wood stock; drill ⅜"-deep hole in each foot where indicated. Sand feet until smooth. Paint feet and dowels orange, adding a second coat if

necessary. Glue ends of dowels in holes in feet.

2. Referring to patterns, cut two bodies, reversing one, and four wings, reversing two, from chenille fabric. Cut one wattle and comb from red felt and two beaks from orange felt.

3. Lay body halves together, right sides facing; sandwich edges of comb, wattle and beaks between body edges, making sure felt pieces point to inside (so they will be outside in their proper position when chicken is turned right side out). Secure with pins as necessary.

4. Using matching thread, sew chicken halves together, stitching with a ¼"–½" seam allowance and leaving a 2" opening at bottom. Turn chicken right side out through opening; stuff with polyester fiberfill and sew opening closed. With scissors, cut fringe in comb and wattle to within about ¼" of body. Glue beak halves together with a dot of glue.

5. Place wing halves together in pairs, right sides facing; sew together as for body, leaving opening. Clip curves as needed and turn wings right side out. Stuff lightly with fiberfill and sew openings closed.

6. Thread long doll needle with thread. Attach ½" buttons for eyes, sewing from one button through to other button and pulling thread snugly. Knot thread and clip ends.

7. Position wings on sides of body and 1" buttons over wings where indicated; attach wings and buttons to chicken, sewing from one side through to the other side, pulling thread so buttons make indentations in wings. Knot thread and clip ends close.

8. Carefully cut two small slits in bottom of chicken where legs should be attached; apply glue to ends of legs and insert through slits into chicken; apply glue as necessary to close slits around dowels.

Options

1. If you don't have access to a scroll saw, make feet from felt and cardboard instead: Cut four feet from orange felt and four corrugated cardboard feet slightly smaller than the felt ones. Glue cardboard feet together in pairs; sandwich between felt feet and glue felt together around edges. Glue assembled feet to bottoms of dowels.

2. For sitting chicken, cut a gusset from chenille in addition to the other pieces. Cut also two bases from corrugated cardboard; glue them together. When stitching chicken together, insert gusset between dots on pattern. When stuffing the chicken, insert fiberfill, then slip in cardboard base and position at chicken's breast, where it will "sit." Add some beans or doll pellets for weight, if desired. Sew opening closed.

3. For legs, make two 10"-long tubes from orange felt, sewing or gluing edges together. Tie knots in tubes where "knees" should be. Glue one end of legs to tops of felt-and-cardboard feet; cut two small slits in base of chicken and insert ends of legs through slits; glue to secure. ◾

Flower Pot Graduates

Celebrating a graduation in your family? Include these charming decorations made from tiny terra-cotta flower pots. Choose paint and floss colors to match the cap and gown worn by your special grad.

Design by Angie Wilhite

Materials

Each Favor

- 1¾"-diameter terra-cotta flower pot
- Wooden products from Forster Inc.:
  1¼" small wooden head bead
  1" wooden doll pin stand
  1½" Woodsies wooden square
- ⅞" wooden bowl
- 2 (4") squares light blue fabric
- 4" square Pellon Heavy-Duty Wonder-Under transfer web
- 4" square Pellon Fusible Fleece
- 6" piece of ⅛"-wide blue satin ribbon
- 6-strand embroidery floss: light blue and royal blue
- Royal blue chenille stem
- Miniature diploma
- 2 (7mm) round black movable eyes
- Curly doll hair
- Satin interior spray #07202 from Delta Technical Coatings Inc.
- Ceramcoat acrylic paints from Delta Technical Coatings Inc.:
  Fleshtone #2019
  Opaque blue #2508
- Paintbrush
- Fine-line black permanent marking pen
- Aleene's Ultimate glue gun and jewelry glue sticks
- Iron

Project Notes

Allow paints and finishes to dry thoroughly between coats.

Refer to photo throughout.

Instructions

1. Following manufacturer's instructions, spray flower pot, doll pin stand, head bead, wooden square and wooden bowl with satin interior spray. Paint head bead fleshtone; paint other pieces opaque blue. Spray again with satin interior spray.

2. Following manufacturer's instructions, fuse fleece to back of one fabric square and transfer web to back of the other. Remove paper backing; sandwich fabric pieces together, web facing fleece, and fuse. Referring to pattern, cut one collar from fused fabric.

3. Cut three 4½" pieces from each color of embroidery floss; cut an additional 5" piece light blue. Fold 4½" pieces in half; wrap 5" piece around folded floss ½" from fold. Knot and trim ends. Glue tassel to top of wooden square for mortarboard.

4. Cut two 3¼" lengths from chenille stem; fold one end of each up ⅜" and other end up 1⅛".

5. Set flower pot upside down. Glue doll pin stand atop flower pot. Glue collar over doll pin stand with notch in front. Glue head atop collar.

6. Cut curls from doll hair and glue to wooden head. Glue bowl upside down on top of head, and mortarboard atop bowl.

7. Tie ribbon in bow; trim ends and glue bow to collar just above notch. Glue eyes to head and draw on smile with marking pen. Glue ⅜" ends of chenille stems to sides of flower pot for arms; glue diploma to one hand. ◼

Patriotic Plant Pokes

Wouldn't Fourth of July picnic tables look great decked out in green plants dressed up with these characters? The designs can easily be adapted to make magnets or lapel pins — or add to a loop of ribbon for a colorful napkin ring!

Designs by Angie Wilhite

Materials

Both Designs

- Rainbow Felt Classics from Kunin Felt:
  2 (4" x 6") pieces cashmere tan #884
  2 (5") squares steel gray #902
- 1 yard (⅝"-wide) red, white and blue grosgrain ribbon
- Pellon Wonder-Under transfer web:
  4" x 6" rectangle
  5" square
- Pellon Fusible Fleece:
  4" x 6" rectangle
  5" square
- 2 wooden jumbo craft sticks from Forster Inc.
- Fire red #2083 Ceramcoat acrylic paint from Delta Technical Coatings Inc.
- Sponge paintbrush
- Exterior varnish from Delta Technical Coatings Inc.
- Black 6-strand embroidery floss
- Embroidery needle
- 4 (10mm) round black movable eyes
- Air-soluble pen
- Aleene's glues by Duncan Enterprises:
  OK to Wash-It fabric glue
  Jewel-It glue
- Iron

Project Notes

Refer to photo throughout.

Allow paint and varnish to dry thoroughly between coats.

Instructions

1. Paint craft sticks red. Add a second coat, if necessary. Coat painted craft sticks with varnish.

2. Following manufacturer's instructions, fuse 4" x 6" piece fusible fleece to back of one piece tan felt and 5" square to back of one gray felt square. Fuse transfer web to backs of remaining felt pieces. Remove paper backing; sandwich tan and gray felt pieces together in pairs, web facing fleece, and fuse.

3. Referring to patterns (page 169), trace one elephant onto gray felt, and one donkey head and two ears, reversing one, onto tan felt. Cut out.

4. Using 3 strands embroidery floss, blanket stitch around all pieces.

5. Using fabric glue, glue ears to back of donkey's head. Using jewel glue, glue eyes to both heads; glue heads to tops of craft sticks.

6. Cut ribbon in half; tie each piece in a bow and glue one to each craft stick. ◼

Happy Home Pot Holders

Haul out your stash of fabric scraps and warm up that sewing machine!
In no time flat you can transform an inexpensive, nondescript pot holder
from the "bargain bin" into a personalized kitchen decor accent!

Design by Helen Rafson

Materials

Each Pot Holder

- Plain 7" pot holder
- 8" square of print fabric or pieces of several different fabrics
- Fusible webbing
- Matching sewing threads
- Matching 6-strand cotton embroidery floss
- Hand-sewing needle
- Sewing machine with zigzag attachment
- Iron

Pattern Notes

Refer to photo throughout for placement. Note that you may choose to cut windows and doors from fabric, as shown on multicolored example, or leave these pieces open, as shown on single-color example.

Instructions

1. Following manufacturer's instructions, fuse webbing to wrong side of fabric(s). Referring to pattern (page 82), trace pattern pieces onto webbing as desired and cut out.

2. Peel off paper backing and fuse fabric pieces onto pot holder.

3. Using matching thread, machine-appliqué around each pattern piece, adding machine-stitched "window-panes" and bottom of door.

4. Set machine for a more open zigzag stitch and zigzag around outer border of pot holder in desired color.

5. Thread sewing machine with thread to match pot holder and set machine for a short, straight stitch. Top-stitch around house ⅛" from edge of house.

6. Using 12 strands embroidery floss, add a French knot "doorknob."

Happy Home Pot Holder

Flower Fairy Wand

This lovely miss makes an enchanting addition to a silk flower arrangement or a houseplant. Little girls would love her all on her own!

Design by Judy Atwell

Materials

- 14½"-diameter wooden dowel
- Porcelain doll head-and-arms set
- 14" piece twisted style braid for hair
- 1 yard ³⁄₁₆"-wide white picot-edge satin ribbon
- 1 yard ⅛"-wide satin ribbon in accent color
- 18" piece 1½"-wide white lace trim
- 4" x 24" strip white net
- 4 (3") white silk roses
- A few white silk rosebuds
- 4 large silk rose leaves
- 9–10 (2") silk accent flowers with leaves
- 16 (½") silk accent flowers
- Gold spray paint
- Hot-glue gun and glue sticks
- Wire cutters

Instructions

1. Spray dowel with gold paint; set aside to dry.

2. Gently untwist and separate braid for hair. Using wire cutters, cut all silk flowers and leaves from their stems; lay out on work surface.

3. Twist net strip; glue one end at top of dowel. Wind net tightly around length of dowel to bottom; secure with glue and trim any excess.

4. Apply hair for braid to doll's head in a spiral, starting at outside edges and leaving a 2" piece of braid hanging over doll's shoulder; work toward center. Using glue sparingly, glue braid over porcelain hair. Cut the braid at top of head off to one side and secure with glue. Glue a few ½" accent flowers over this spot.

5. Using glue gun, pleat lace trim as you attach it to base of doll's shoulder head, beginning in back. Glue doll head to top of dowel; stuff with scraps of net if it is too loose.

6. Form shoulders by gluing a white silk rose into each shoulder socket under the lace. Glue another white rose to front of dowel under doll's chest, and glue fourth white rose to back of dowel under lace.

7. Cut scraps of lace trim and glue around porcelain arms as for sleeves. Glue each arm into the center of a flat 2" accent flower. Glue arms into centers of each shoulder rose.

8. Position two large rose leaves high on each side of doll's back and glue in place, making sure right sides of leaves face front. Glue 2" accent flower where leaves meet in back.

9. Glue some 2" accent flowers to front between lace and front rose. To finish bottom, glue accent flowers, starting with 2" flat ones, around bottom of roses. Fill in additional spaces with ½" accent flowers and rosebuds.

10. Tuck two or three small green leaves, cut from accent flowers, at very bottom of flowers. Fold ribbons in half; lift leaves and glue folded ends of ribbons to dowel; press leaves down and glue over ribbon ends. ▪

Just for Kids

Perfect for filling up a rainy day at home or an active day at school, each of these exciting crafts for kids is sure to bring hours of hands-on fun!

Blooming Bubble Blowers!

Introduce youngsters to the special satisfaction of using "recycled" materials with these cute designs. Once the "bubble juice" is gone, the bubble wands become the basis for these fun and simple designs.

Designs by Angie Wilhite

Materials

Both Blooms

- Pink and yellow recycled plastic bubble wands
- 2 (¾"-diameter) wooden furniture buttons
- Woodsies wooden shapes from Forster Inc.:
  2 medium (¾") circles
  10 medium (1½"-long) teardrops
- Americana multipurpose sealer #DS17 from DecoArt
- Americana acrylic paints from DecoArt:
  Cadmium yellow #DA10
  Baby pink #DA31
  Kelly green #DA55
- Paintbrush
- Black fine-point permanent marking pen
- 4 (7mm) round black wiggly eyes
- Gem-Tac adhesive from Beacon Adhesives
- Autumn and Strawberry Curly Hair from One & Only Creations
- ½ yard (⅛"-wide) kelly green satin ribbon
- 2" cube plastic foam
- 1⅞" terra-cotta flowerpot
- 7" piece carnation pink ribbon scroll #8002 from C.M. Offray & Son

Project Notes

Refer to photo throughout.

Let all paints, finishes and ink dry before applying additional coats or layers.

Flowerpot Bloom

1. Apply sealer to one furniture button and five teardrops. Paint teardrops baby pink and furniture button cadmium yellow.

2. Draw mouth on furniture button and glue on two wiggly eyes.

3. Arrange teardrops in shape of flower, pointed ends in center. Lay wooden circle over center of teardrop "petals"; glue to secure.

4. Glue furniture button to rough circle of pink bubble wand; glue teardrop flower to back of rough circle.

5. Cut 3" strand of curly hair; glue over top of wooden button. Tie green ribbon in bow around stem of bubble wand.

6. Cut plastic foam to fit snugly inside flowerpot. Remove craft foam; paint it kelly green and let dry. Return painted foam to flowerpot.

7. Cut unused circle end off bubble wand. Apply a little glue to cut end and insert in foam in pot.

8. Glue ribbon scroll around rim of flowerpot, overlapping ends in back.

"Long-Stem Beauty" Bloom

Follow steps 1–5 for Flowerpot Bloom, using yellow bubble wand and painting petals cadmium yellow. ◉

Nuts About Animals!

Walnut shells cleverly give dimension to this trio of easy-to-craft critters.
Complete them with scraps of felt, then add a pin back or a magnet.

Designs by Kathy Wegner

Project Note

Refer to photo throughout.

Chick

1. Paint walnut shell yellow; let dry.

2. Referring to patterns (page 170), lay walnut shell on pattern for chick body; adjusting for differences in size and shape, cut one body from yellow felt; cut chick feet from orange felt.

3. Stuff cotton ball into walnut shell. Applying glue to edge of shell, glue shell to yellow felt; glue orange feet to base of shell.

4. Sew pin to back of felt, or press on adhesive-backed magnet.

5. Glue two seed beads to head for eyes; paint beak with orange shiny fabric paint. Spray with matte varnish if desired.

Bunny

1. Referring to pattern (page 170), lay unpainted walnut shell on pattern for bunny; adjusting for differences in size and shape, cut one body from tan felt.

2. Stuff cotton ball into walnut shell. Applying glue to edge of shell, glue shell to tan felt; glue white pompom to shell for tail.

Materials

All Animals

- 3 (1⅝"-long) walnut shell halves
- Felt scraps: yellow, orange, tan and black
- Acrylic craft paints: yellow and red
- Shiny fabric paints: orange and pale peach
- Small paintbrush
- 3 black seed beads
- 2 (3mm) round black wiggle eyes
- 5mm pompoms:
  1 white
  6 black
- 3 cotton balls or equal amounts polyester fiberfill
- 3 (1") safety pins, pin backs or sections of ½"-wide adhesive-backed magnet strip
- Hand-sewing needle and coordinating threads
- Tacky craft glue
- Matte-finish spray varnish (optional)

3. Sew pin to back of felt, or press on adhesive-backed magnet.

4. Glue one seed bead to head for eye; paint nose and inside of ear with pale peach shiny fabric paint. Spray with matte varnish if desired.

Ladybug

1. Paint walnut shell red; let dry.

2. Referring to pattern (page 170), lay walnut shell on pattern for ladybug; adjusting for differences in size and shape, cut one ladybug from black felt.

3. Stuff cotton ball into walnut shell. Applying glue to edge of shell, glue shell to black felt. Glue black pompoms to shell.

4. Sew pin to back of felt, or press on adhesive-backed magnet.

5. Glue wiggly eyes to head. Spray with matte varnish if desired. ✿

All-Star Photo Frame

Preserve championship memories in this simply constructed frame! Encourage young crafters to be creative by substituting a special statistic, score or their name on one of the stars, or by incorporating team colors and names in this versatile design.

Design by Janna Britton

Materials

- Woodsies wooden shapes from Forster Inc.:
  4 small (⅜") circles
  4 medium (¾") circles
  4 large (1¼") circles
  4 large (1½") stars
- 4 wooden craft sticks from Forster Inc.
- Americana acrylic paints from DecoArt:
  White wash #DA2
  Pumpkin #DA13
  Lamp (ebony) black #DA67
  Primary yellow #DA201
- Gold metallic spray paint
- Tulip white slick dimensional fabric paint from Duncan Enterprises
- Paintbrushes: ½" flat and #1 liner
- Black extra-fine-point permanent marking pen
- Waxed paper
- Aleene's Ultimate glue gun and jewelry glue sticks by Duncan Enterprises
- 4 (1") sections ½"-wide adhesive-back magnet strip

Project Notes

Refer to photo throughout.

Paint fronts and edges of all wooden pieces unless instructed otherwise.

Let all paints, sealer and ink dry before applying adjacent or overlaying paints, ink, or glue.

Instructions

1. Cover work surface with waxed paper. Using ½" paintbrush and white wash, base-coat all small circles (golf balls), two medium circles (baseballs) and two large circles (soccer balls). Using pumpkin, base-coat two large circles (basketballs); using primary yellow, base-coat two medium circles (tennis balls). Spray all stars with gold paint.

2. Referring to patterns (page 170) and using marking pen, add seam lines and stitches to baseballs; draw lines on basketballs; dot dimples onto all golf balls; draw pattern onto soccer balls.

3. Fill in solid sections on soccer balls using #1 liner and black paint. Using white slick dimensional fabric paint, draw seam lines on yellow tennis balls. Using marking pen, write "All Star" on each star.

4. Arrange craft sticks in a square frame and glue at corners. Glue star in center of each side. Glue golf balls, tennis balls and baseballs beside stars; glue soccer balls and basketballs in corners.

5. Press magnet pieces onto back of frame at corners, making sure magnets do not show from front. Glue or tape photo to wrong side of frame. ☕

Bunny & Bear Picture Frame

Craft sticks have been prime crafting material since way back when! Today's young crafters can take advantage of lots of wooden cutout shapes that are fun to arrange and easy to work with.

Design by Janna Britton

Materials

- Woodsies wooden shapes from Forster Inc.:
  9 large (1¼") circles
  1 medium (¾") circle
  5 small (⅜") circles
  6 medium (1½"-long) teardrops
  2 small (⅞"-long) teardrops
- 4 wooden craft sticks from Forster Inc.
- Americana acrylic paints from DecoArt:
  White wash #DA2
  Kelly green #DA55
  Lamp (ebony) black #DA67
  Sapphire #DA99
  Honey brown #DA163
  Santa red #DA170
- Tulip pearl dimensional fabric paints from Duncan Enterprises: pink and buttercup
- Tulip white slick dimensional fabric paint from Duncan Enterprises
- ½" flat paintbrush
- Sharp craft knife or heavy-duty craft scissors
- Black extra-fine-point permanent marking pen
- Clear acrylic spray sealer
- Waxed paper
- Aleene's Ultimate glue gun and jewelry glue sticks by Duncan Enterprises
- 4 (1") sections ½"-wide adhesive-back magnet strip

Project Notes

Refer to photo throughout.

Paint fronts and edges of all wooden pieces unless instructed otherwise.

Let all paints, sealer and ink dry before applying adjacent or overlaying paints, ink, sealer or glue.

Painting

1. Cover work surface with waxed paper. For balloons, base-coat one large circle with Santa red, one with sapphire and one with kelly green.

2. For bear, base-coat three large circles, one medium circle, three small circles and four medium teardrops with honey brown.

3. For bunny, cut one small circle in half with craft knife. Using white wash, base-coat halves, another small circle, two large circles, two medium teardrops and two small teardrops.

4. Referring to pattern for ball (page 89), paint sections of remaining large circle with white wash, Santa red, sapphire and kelly green.

5. Base-coat one entire craft stick and about 1" of the end of another craft stick with kelly green.

Assembly

1. On work surface, lay one unpainted craft stick on the left and green-tipped craft stick on the right, green tip toward bottom. Make frame by gluing another unpainted craft stick across top, matching ends, and painted green craft stick across bottom.

2. Glue balloons together, overlapping as shown; glue balloons to top left corner of frame.

3. Referring to pattern for bear, glue three large circles together, overlapping top and bottom circles over center as shown. Glue medium circle to head, positioning it toward bottom of head. Atop medium circle, glue one small circle, positioning it toward top of medium circle. Glue remaining small circles to wrong side of head for ears, and pointed ends of medium teardrops to wrong side of body for arms and legs. Dip tip of paintbrush handle into ebony paint and dot eyes onto large circle and nose onto small circle. Glue teddy bear to right side of frame.

4. Referring to pattern for bunny, glue two large circles together, overlapping edge of top circle (head) slightly over bottom circle (body). Glue small whole circle to head for nose and mouth; glue halves of small circle to body front for paws. Glue pointed ends of two medium teardrops to back of head for ears; glue pointed ends of two small teardrops top bottom of body for feet. Dip tip of paintbrush handle into ebony paint and dot eyes onto large circle and nose onto small circle. Glue bunny to left side of frame.

Bunny

Bear

5. Glue ball to bottom front of frame at right, overlapping teddy bear's foot slightly.

Finishing

1. Spray frame front with sealer.

2. Paint highlight on each balloon using white slick dimensional fabric paint.

3. With marking pen, add detail lines to teddy bear's ears and draw mouth below nose; draw dashed line around medium circle on head, and around legs and arms, adding markings for paws.

4. With marking pen, draw whiskers and mouth on small circle on bunny; add marks to paws and feet. Paint insides of ears with pink pearl dimensional fabric paint.

5. Add a dot of buttercup pearl dimensional fabric paint to ball where four colors meet.

6. Press magnet pieces onto back of frame, making sure magnets do not show from front. Glue or tape photo to wrong side of frame. 🌀

Sapphire

Kelly Green

Santa Red

White Wash

Ball

Noah's Ark Stand-ups

Imagine the feeling of accomplishment when your youngsters make their own toys!
They'll enjoy helping to color the animals as much as playing with the completed play set.

Design by Judith Barker for American Traditional Stencils

Materials

- 20" x 30" piece stiff card stock or poster board
- American Traditional Stencils:
  Noah's Ark #BL 710
  Noah's Animals #BL 711
  Mrs. Noah #BL 712
- Coloring materials of your choice: poster paints, acrylic paints, oil paint sticks, colored pencils or markers, etc.
- ³⁄₁₆" stencil brush or other applicator for your coloring material
- Craft glue or double-sided tape
- Low-tack masking tape
- Large piece blue poster board (optional)

Instructions

1. Referring to instructions that accompany stencils, use masking tape to tape stencil to card stock or white poster board; mask any areas you do not want to color.

2. Apply paints sparingly with dry brush, blending as desired to create shading and wiping off excess so it does not seep under stencil. If using another coloring method, trace around the stencil, remove stencil and color in figure as desired. Let all colors dry thoroughly.

3. Referring to photo throughout, carefully trim around top and sides of design leaving ¹⁄₈" margin. Cut straight across bottom leaving ¼"–½" margin.

4. Referring to easel pattern (page 170), cut easels from card stock, cutting as many as necessary to support each piece, and adjusting sizes to fit. Some stand-ups can be supported by a single easel; larger pieces will require two or three to hold them steadily.

5. Fold easels along dotted line; glue or tape flat tab to back of each stand-up. Use blue poster board as a backdrop for the stand-ups, if desired. ◉

Cute as a Bug Puppets

Younger crafters will have fun creating a whole bevy of beautiful bugs from felt scraps and other crafting staples. It's a fun way to keep fingers busy and safely out of trouble.

Designs by Sandy Dye

Materials

- CPE felt:
  Black felt
  Red, yellow and orange Eazy Felt
- 2 (3mm) black round cabochons
- 4 (3mm) black pompoms
- Chenille stems: black and lime green
- ¼" and ⅛" round hole punches
- Thick, clear-drying craft glue

Project Note

Refer to photo throughout.

Ladybug

1. Referring to patterns (page 171), cut one body along solid outline and one underbody along dashed line from black felt; cut two wings, reversing one, from red felt.

2. Glue long edges of underbody to bottom of body to make pocket for finger, leaving front and back open.

3. Using ¼" hole punch, punch 18 circles from black felt; glue to right sides of wings. Glue wings to body.

4. For antennae, cut 3" section from black chenille stem; bend into a V. Glue pompom to each end of V; glue base of V under ladybug inside pocket, leaving about ½" antennae protruding from front of ladybug.

5. Glue cabochons to head for eyes.

Flying Bug

1. Referring to patterns (page 171), cut one body from black felt, one wing piece from yellow felt and one wing piece from orange felt.

2. Fold body into a tube for finger and glue edges together.

3. Cut three 1½" pieces from black chenille stem; bend each into a squarish U. Glue pairs of legs to bottom of body, applying glue to bases of U's so legs extend downward.

4. Using ¼" hole punch, punch two circles from red felt; glue to head for eyes. Cut a tiny smile from red felt and glue below eyes.

5. Using ⅛" hole punch, punch two black circles, eight yellow circles and 10 red circles. Glue black circles atop red eyes; glue red circles evenly spaced over yellow wings; glue yellow circles in clusters of four to orange wings. Glue wings to top of body.

6. For antennae, cut 3" section from lime green chenille stem; bend into a V, bending tips out slightly. Glue pompom to each end of V; glue base of V under bug inside pocket, leaving about ½" antennae protruding from front of bug. ◉

Busy Bee Plant Poke

Working with craft foam is fun and easy! Let your young crafter make one of these bees to include in your next gift bouquet—or substitute a small piece of adhesive-backed magnet for the plant poke, and slip a couple "busy bees" in your next letter to Grandma!

Design by Jackie Haskell

Busy Bee Wing
Cut 2 from white craft foam

Busy Bee Body
Cut 1 from yellow craft foam

Materials

- Craft foam: yellow, white and black
- Pink powdered cosmetic blusher
- Cotton-tip swab
- 2 (7mm) round black wiggly eyes
- Tiny bow of ⅛"-wide purple ribbon
- 2 (5mm) black pompoms
- Wooden skewer
- Black ultra-fine-point permanent marking pen
- Clear-drying craft glue

Project Notes

Refer to photo throughout.

Wooden skewers have sharp points! Keep pointed skewers away from young children. Adults may wish to help with final step of assembly. Or, substitute a plastic drinking straw for the skewer.

Instructions

1. Referring to patterns, cut one body from yellow craft foam and two wings from white craft foam.

2. Glue points of wings to wrong side of bee body. Cut three long, thin stripes from black craft foam; glue to body and trim any extra foam from ends.

3. Glue eyes in place. Cut tiny yellow foam oval and glue, centered, below eyes for nose.

4. For cheeks, use cotton-tipped swab to rub a small amount of powdered blusher onto yellow foam below each eye. Using marking pen, draw on smile and tiny lines at corners of eyes.

5. For antennae, cut two narrow, ¾"-long strips from black craft foam; glue pompom to end of each and glue other end to wrong side of head.

6. Glue bow off to one side at top of head; glue blunt end of skewer to back of bee. ◉

Blossoming Brooch

This project is as easy as punching holes! Colorful circles of craft foam are arranged to make flowers, and a single red dot becomes a friendly ladybug on a pin that will dress up any spring outfit.

Design by Jackie Haskell

Materials

- Craft foam: black, light green, royal blue, purple and red
- ¼" round hole punch
- 3 (5mm) yellow pompoms
- 1" pin back
- Black ultra-fine-point permanent marking pen
- Pinking shears
- Sharp craft knife
- Mini hot-glue gun with narrow nozzle

Instructions

1. Referring to pattern below, cut one background from light green craft foam using pinking shears.

2. Punch 10 circles from royal blue craft foam, five circles from purple, one circle from red and one from black.

3. Arrange five royal blue foam circles in a ring, edges touching, to make five-petal flower. Glue petals together, applying tiny amounts of glue to edges of petals. Repeat with remaining royal blue and purple foam circles. Glue yellow pompom in center of each flower.

4. Cut a straight slice equal to about one-quarter of foam circle from edge of red foam circle. Cut black circle in half; glue straight edge of one black half to straight edge of larger red piece, applying glue to edges only.

5. Using marking pen, define ladybug wings with a single straight line down center of red foam dot; add three black dots to each red wing. On flower petals, draw radiant lines from yellow center.

6. Glue flowers to light green foam background with purple flower in center; glue ladybug overlapping edges of purple and one royal blue flower. Glue pin back to back of light green craft foam. ✿

Blossoming Brooch Background
Cut 1 from light green craft foam
using pinking shears

Wrapping-Paper Bookmark

This simple project offers boundless creative potential! The littlest crafters who still have trouble manipulating scissors accurately can safely embellish bookmarks with stickers instead of cutout stars.

Design by Helen L. Rafson

Materials

- 2½" x 7" strip white art paper
- Wrapping paper
- Glue stick
- Pinking shears or pattern-edge scissors (optional)
- Clear contact paper
- ¼" round hole punch
- 5 (10") strands embroidery floss in coordinating color

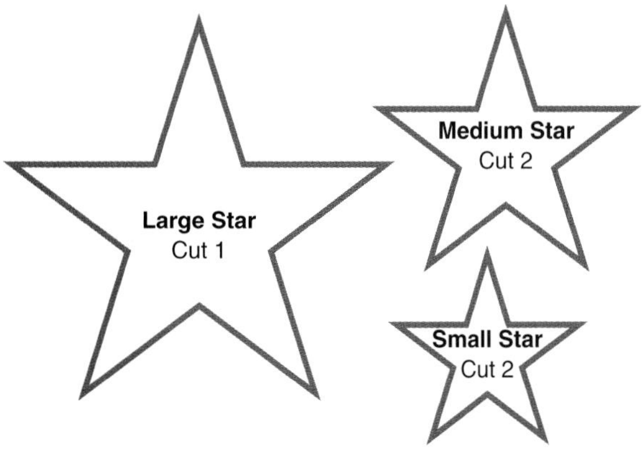

Large Star
Cut 1

Medium Star
Cut 2

Small Star
Cut 2

Project Note

Refer to photo throughout.

Instructions

1. Referring to patterns, cut one large star, two medium stars and two small stars from wrapping paper.

2. Also from wrapping paper, cut two strips ¼" x 7" and two strips ¼" x 2½". Glue these strips to art paper to make border around bookmark. Trim edges of bookmark with pinking shears or pattern-edge scissors, if desired.

3. Glue stars to front of bookmark.

4. Cut two pieces of contact paper 4½" x 9". Lay bookmark in center of one piece; cover with second piece of contact paper. Press with fingers to secure layers. Trim excess contact paper, leaving ⅛" border all around bookmark.

5. Punch hole at center top of bookmark. Hold embroidery floss strands together, ends even. Fold strands in half. Pull uncut end through hole; pass cut ends through loop and pull gently to secure knot. Trim tassel ends evenly. ◉

#1 Teacher Ornament

Youngsters will enjoy giving their teachers something they made themselves—and teachers will treasure it, too! This ornament is appropriate for year-round display.

Design by Barbara A. Woolley

Materials

- 4½"-wide section of 5½"-tall wooden fence
- 2"-wide wooden heart cutout
- 1" x 1½" wooden rectangle
- Round wooden toothpick
- 1"-tall wooden school bell
- 1½"-wide x 1¼"-tall wooden open book
- Small happy face from True Colors International's Faces for Places
- Acrylic paints: red, white, black, brown, green and metallic gold
- Paintbrushes: liner and #10 multipurpose
- White extra-fine-line marking pen
- Small clump doll hair or yarn
- 12" piece 12-gauge craft wire
- 1" flat wooden button
- 12" piece (½"-wide) navy blue grosgrain ribbon
- Craft drill with ⅛" bit
- Hot-glue gun and glue sticks

Project Notes

Refer to photo throughout.

Let paints and inks dry between coats.

Instructions

1. Thin white acrylic paint with water. Using multipurpose brush for all painting through first part of step 6, whitewash fence with thinned mixture, wiping off most of the paint with a paper towel. Repeat as desired to attain preferred color. Drill a hole in upper corner of each side of top crosspiece for attaching hanger later.

2. Paint heart red on both sides. Write "#1 TEACHER" on front using white extra-fine-line marker.

3. Paint rectangle black for slate; paint brown frame around slate on front and edges. Write sum and simple words on black portion of slate using white extra-fine-point marker.

4. Cut a ½" piece from one end of toothpick; cut off sharp point. Paint white and glue to upper right corner of slate for slate chalk.

5. Paint bell handle black; paint bell metallic gold.

6. Paint book white; paint cover green. Using liner brush and black paint, add words of your choice to pages, and paint little characters in book as desired.

7. Glue hair around face. Cut ribbon in half; tie each piece in a bow and glue one to bottom edge of face.

8. Glue heart to upper left portion of fence; glue bell at center top, atop crosspiece; glue slate with chalk to top right. Glue book to fence at bottom left and face at bottom right.

9. Thread wire through button; secure button in center, coiling wire ends around paintbrush handle or pencil, then sliding coils off and stretching them as desired. Glue remaining ribbon bow to button front over wire. Thread ends of wire through holes in fence. ❦

Every Day's a Holiday

*Make every holiday extra-special
and extra-fun with fun and festive
decorations and gifts to share
with family and friends!*

Candlelit Seasons

It's said that everything—and everyone—looks better in candlelight. That certainly applies to these recycled bottles! A combination of easy etching and painting techniques transforms them into the stars of your holiday table!

Designs by Annie Lang

Materials

Each Candle Holder

- 9"-tall bottle, empty and clean
- 6"–8" candle in coordinating color
- 12" piece (⅛"- to ¼"-wide) satin ribbon in coordinating color
- 2" round crocheted doily
- Dip n Etch etching dip from B&B Products
- Expression paintbrushes from Daler-Rowney/Robert Simmons:
  Series E60 flat shader #10
  Series E85 pointed round #2 and #4
  Series E51 liner #0 and #1
- #0 Rapidograph pen from Koh-I-Noor
- UltraDraw Waterproof black India ink
- Craft glue
- Plastic pitcher

Spring Eggs

- Americana acrylic paints from DecoArt:
  Titanium white #DA1
  Cadmium orange #DA14
  Calico red #DA20
  Baby pink #DA31
  True blue #DA36
  Baby blue #DA42
  Lamp black #DA67
  Primary yellow #DA201

Summer Flowers

- Americana acrylic paints from DecoArt:
  Titanium white #DA1
  Cadmium orange #DA14
  Calico red #DA20
  Baby pink #DA31
  True blue #DA36
  Baby blue #DA42
  Dark pine #DA49
  Bright green #DA54
  Lamp black #DA67
  Primary yellow #DA201

Autumn Leaves

- Americana acrylic paints from DecoArt:
  Titanium white #DA1
  Cadmium orange #DA14
  Calico red #DA20
  Lamp black #DA67
  Primary yellow #DA201

Peppermint Candy

- Americana acrylic paints from DecoArt:
  Titanium white #DA1
  Calico red #DA20
  Baby blue #DA42
  Dark pine #DA49
  Bright green #DA54

Project Notes

Carefully read instructions for etching dip before beginning.

Any small bottles can be recycled for these projects. For additional color, fill bottles with colored sand, decorative marbles, etc.

Refer to photo throughout.

Preparation

1. Following manufacturer's instructions, pour etching dip into plastic pitcher. Place bottle in etching dip. Wait 15 minutes, then remove bottle from dip and rinse under running water.

2. Referring to patterns (page 172), sketch or trace desired pattern on bottle four times around bottom of bottle, spacing motifs evenly and overlapping or touching motifs as necessary.

Spring Eggs

1. Paint one egg titanium white; apply a little baby blue shading around edges of egg to add dimension. Paint bow baby pink; shade with thinned calico red.

2. Using round brushes, fill in mouth with lamp black, tongue with baby pink, paint nose calico red, add two small black eyes, then two baby pink wavy lines near top of egg. Thin calico red with water and tap some color onto cheek areas.

3. Using liner brush, add titanium white highlights to cheeks and bow.

4. Using pen and India ink, outline entire egg and add details.

5. Repeat steps 1–4 on second egg, painting egg baby blue and shading with true blue. Bow is primary yellow, shaded with cadmium orange.

6. Repeat steps 1–4 on third egg, painting egg baby pink and shading with thinned calico red. Bow is titanium white, shaded with baby blue.

7. Repeat steps 1–4 on fourth egg, painting egg primary yellow and shading with a little cadmium

orange. Bow is baby blue, shaded with true blue.

Summer Flowers

1. Paint flower faces primary yellow; float edges with a little cadmium orange. Paint petals with titanium white; apply a little baby blue shading. Paint bows baby blue; shade with true blue. Paint stems and leaves bright green with dark pine shading.

2. Using round brushes, fill in mouths with lamp black, tongue with baby pink, paint noses calico red, and add small black eyes. Thin calico red with water and tap some color onto cheek areas.

3. Using liner brush, add titanium white highlights to cheeks and bows.

4. Using pen and India ink, outline entire flower and add details.

Autumn Leaves

1. Paint first and third leaves primary yellow; float edges with a little cadmium orange. Paint bow cadmium orange; apply a little thinned calico red for shading.

2. Paint second and fourth leaves cadmium orange; shade with thinned calico red. Paint bow primary yellow; shade with cadmium orange.

3. Using round brushes, fill in mouths with lamp black, tongue with baby pink, paint noses calico red, and add small black eyes. Thin calico red with water and tap some color onto cheek areas.

4. Using liner brush, add titanium white highlights to cheeks and bows.

5. Using pen and India ink, outline leaves and add details.

Peppermint Candy

1. Paint canes titanium white; float border edges with baby blue. Using flat brush, add calico red stripes.

2. Paint bows bright green; add dark pine shading.

3. Using liner brush, add titanium white highlight lines down each cane and onto bow.

4. Using pen and India ink, outline and add details.

Finishing

1. Snip center from doily so it will slip over threaded mouth of bottle. Secure doily with a touch of glue if necessary.

2. Insert candle in neck of bottle, shaving end of candle if necessary to make it fit snugly.

3. Tie satin ribbon around bottle neck in a bow. ◗

"Loves Me" Card

"He loves me, he loves me not, he loves me. …" We all have probably tried to chart
true love's course with this little verse; how annoying when the flower doesn't cooperate! Your sweetheart
is sure to respond lovingly when you present this handmade token of your affection.

Design by Laura Scott

Materials

- 5" x 7" Paper Reflections off-white paper by DMD Industries
- 5" x 7" Paper Reflections off-white card and envelope by DMD Industries
- He Loves Me stamp #7024AC by Craft Stamps
- Black ink pad
- Fine-point marking pens: fuchsia, lime green, emerald green, turquoise, dark turquoise, yellow and black
- Red watercolor paint
- Large plastic plate
- Double-sided adhesive tape

Project Note

Refer to photo throughout.

Instructions

1. Center stamp on paper. Color in stamp as desired or using photo as a guide.

2. Gently tear away approximately ¼" from each edge of paper.

3. Place 2 or 3 drops of red watercolor paint on a large plate. Add ½ teaspoon water and mix well, until paint is a very light red. Carefully dip just the edges of torn paper into paint. Gently rub paint into torn edges with finger. Effect should be very subtle.

4. Using black marking pen, write "Happy Valentine's Day" in capital dot lettering with a dot between each letter across bottom of card.

5. Center and tape stamped paper to front of card above lettering.

Corrugated Heart Brooch

Here's a pleasing alternative to the lacy, frilly hearts that abound around Valentine's Day. Red corrugated paper gives it lots of texture. Sprinkle on a few buttons and a faux-antique gold charm, and you have the perfect accent for your denim jumper and other casual fashions.

Design by Kathy Wegner

Materials
- 3½" square red corrugated paper
- 3½" square tan felt
- ½" "antique gold" heart charm
- 3 buttons, ⅝" diameter or smaller
- 1" pin back
- Tan sewing thread and hand-sewing needle
- 5" piece fine jute twine
- Tacky craft glue

Project Note
Refer to photo throughout.

Instructions

1. Referring to heart pattern below, cut one heart from corrugated paper. Using corrugated heart as a pattern, cut another heart from tan felt, cutting ⅛" larger all around.

2. Sew pin back to felt heart. Sew buttons and charm onto corrugated heart.

3. Tie a tiny bow from twine; glue above charm. Glue corrugated heart to felt heart.

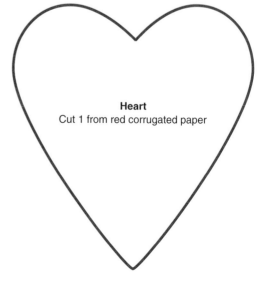

Heart
Cut 1 from red corrugated paper

Valentine Heart Pins

These sweet designs boast charming decorative buttons, felt hearts dressed up with blanket stitch, and ready-made Battenburg lace hearts. What could be simpler?

Designs by Angie Wilhite

Materials

Each Pin

- 2 (4") squares red felt
- 4" white Battenburg lace heart #099-4 from Wimpole Street Creations
- 4" square Pellon Wonder-Under fusible transfer web
- 4" square Pellon Fusible Fleece
- Black 6-strand embroidery floss
- La Mode decorative button from Blumenthal/Lansing Co.: Christmas Stitchery teddy bear #1663, Victorian Romance heart-and-hand #1858 or heart envelope #1859
- Gem-Tac adhesive from Beacon Adhesives
- ¾" pin back
- Iron
- Press cloth

Project Note

Refer to photo throughout.

Instructions

1. Following manufacturer's instructions, fuse transfer web to wrong side of one felt square and fusible fleece to wrong side of other felt square. Lay felt pieces wrong sides facing; cover with press cloth and fuse together.

2. Referring to heart pattern, cut one heart from fused felt layers. Using 3 strands black embroidery floss, Blanket-Stitch around edge of heart.

3. Sew or glue button to center of felt heart. Glue felt heart to center of Battenburg lace heart. Glue pin back to wrong side of Battenburg lace heart.

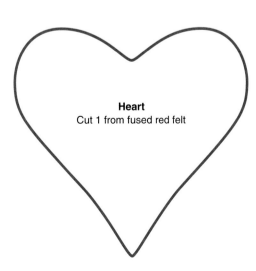

Heart
Cut 1 from fused red felt

Heart & Hand Card

A tan card and envelope and fabrics in a variety of country-style colors, prints and checks give this greeting card a decidedly warm and "down-home" charm.

Design by Angie Wilhite

other square. Lay fabric pieces wrong sides facing; fuse.

2. Referring to patterns below, cut one large heart from fused fabric layers. Using 2 strands gold embroidery floss, Blanket-Stitch around edge of heart.

3. Following manufacturer's instructions, fuse heavy-duty transfer web to wrong side of navy print, burgundy check and remaining burgundy print fabrics. Referring to patterns, cut one hand from navy print, one medium heart and one small heart from burgundy print, and two small hearts from burgundy check. Remove paper backing.

4. Position hand and small burgundy print heart on front of card as shown. Position Blanket-Stitched heart under thumb. Fuse pieces in place (thumb will hold Blanket-Stitched heart in place).

5. Position medium burgundy print heart between small burgundy check hearts on envelope flap; fuse.

6. Using marking pen, outline hand with heart on card and hearts on envelope with simulated "stitching."

Materials

- 5" x 7" tan card and envelope
- 8" square burgundy print fabric
- 5" square burgundy checked fabric
- 6" square navy print fabric
- ⅛ yard Pellon Wonder-Under fusible transfer web
- ⅛ yard Pellon Fusible Fleece
- ⅛ yard Pellon Heavy-Duty Wonder-Under fusible transfer web
- Gold 6-strand embroidery floss
- Black fine-line permanent marking pen
- Iron

Project Note

Refer to photo throughout.

Instructions

1. From burgundy print, cut two 3" squares. Following manufacturer's instructions, fuse transfer web to wrong side of one square and fusible fleece to wrong side of

Hand
Cut 1 from navy print

Small Heart
Cut 2 from burgundy check and 1 from burgundy print

Medium Heart
Cut 1 from burgundy print

Large Heart
Cut 1 from fused burgundy print

St. Pat's Door Decoration

Visitors will know "Irish is spoken here!" when they see this cheerful shamrock on your door. Because it's made of lightweight craft foam, it can also hang from a suction cup on your window, mirror or any smooth surface!

Design by Kathy Wegner

Materials

- Craft foam:
  6" square black
  5" square green
  2½" square white
- Tulip 3-D paints by Duncan Enterprises:
  Slick white #65000
  Slick yellow #65002
- Thick tacky craft glue
- Large blunt needle
- 15" piece 19-gauge black craft wire
- Needle-nose pliers
- Wooden round paintbrush handle, pencil or dowel (optional)

Project Note

Refer to photo throughout.

Instructions

1. Referring to patterns, cut one shamrock from green foam and four flowers from white foam. Glue shamrock to center of black square; glue flower in each corner.

2. Paint centers in flowers with slick yellow paint.

3. Add background flowers randomly to black foam: Dot on centers of yellow slick paint; dot five petals of slick white paint around each center.

4. Using large blunt needle, carefully poke a hole for hanging in each upper corner. Bend wire to curve it; thread ends through holes from back to front. Using needle-nose pliers, twist a coil in both ends of wire. (Or, coil wire end around paintbrush handle.) ❦

Flower
Cut 4 from white craft foam

Shamrock Plaque Shamrock
Cut 1 from green craft foam

St. Pat's Pin & Napkin Ring

Pin a wee bit of the luck o' the Irish to your lapel with this colorful pin made from craft foam.
Sponging a bit of paint onto the craft foam gives the design a textured appearance.
The motif also makes a sweet napkin ring for your St. Patrick's Day table.

Design by Helen L. Rafson

Materials

Each Design
- Craft foam: orange, black, green and peach
- Hold the Foam craft foam glue from Beacon Adhesives
- Acrylic craft paints: orange, black, white and green (see Project Notes)
- Gold-glitter fabric paint
- Paint sponge
- Liner paintbrush
- Toothpick
- Pink powdered cosmetic blusher
- Cotton-tip swab
- ¼" round hole punch
- Black fine-tip permanent marking pen

Pin
- 1" pin back

Napkin Ring
- 1½" ring cut from cardboard paper towel or bathroom tissue tube
- Green acrylic paint to match green craft foam
- ½" paintbrush

Project Notes

Refer to photo throughout.

When choosing orange and green paints for sponging on craft foam, select colors a shade or two darker than the craft foam.

Let all paints dry before applying overlaying coats or glue.

Instructions

1. Referring to patterns (page 173), cut two eyebrows and one beard from orange craft foam; cut one hat from green, one hatband from black, and one face from peach. Also punch one circle from peach for nose.

2. Lightly sponge orange paint onto eyebrows and beard; lightly sponge green paint onto hat. Dip wooden end of paintbrush handle into green paint; dot clusters of three dots onto hat for shamrocks, adding stems with paintbrush.

3. Using gold glitter paint and liner brush, paint buckle on hatband.

4. Dip wooden end of paintbrush handle into black paint; dot on eyes. Add highlights by applying a tiny dot of white paint to each eye with the tip of a toothpick.

5. Draw mouth with marking pen. Apply pink blusher to cheeks with cotton-tip swab.

6. Glue hatband to hat. Glue beard to face, aligning pieces according to dashed lines on patterns; glue on eyebrows and nose. Glue hat to head, overlapping as indicated by dashed lines.

7. For pin, glue pin back to back. For napkin ring, use ½" paintbrush to paint cardboard ring inside and out with acrylic green paint to match green craft foam. Glue foam leprechaun to painted ring. ❧

Shamrock Brooch

Show your Irish spirit with this easy-to-make brooch! It's the perfect touch of green for all your casual fashions.

Design by Kathy Wegner

Materials

- 3½" square green corrugated paper
- 3½" square black felt
- ½" "antique gold" shamrock charm
- 2 buttons
- 1" pin back
- Black sewing thread and hand-sewing needle
- Tacky craft glue

Project Note

Refer to photo throughout.

Instructions

1. Referring to shamrock pattern, cut one shamrock from corrugated paper. Using corrugated shamrock as a pattern, cut another shamrock from black felt, cutting ⅛" larger all around.

2. Sew pin back to felt shamrock. Sew buttons and charm onto corrugated shamrock.

3. Glue corrugated shamrock to felt shamrock. ❧

Shamrock
Cut 1 from green corrugated paper

Sculpted Bunny Basket

Imagine your Easter table or buffet decorated with these little baskets containing colorful sculpted bunnies and eggs! You can adapt the colors to match your table linens. They'll delight guests of all ages!

Design by Jackie Haskell

Materials

- Sculpey III modeling compound:
  Dusty rose #303
  Peach #392
  Ivory brilliant #501
  Turquoise #505
- 2 black seed beads
- 1¼" basket
- Green cellophane Easter grass
- ⅛"-wide mauve ribbon
- Pink powdered cosmetic blusher
- Cotton-tip swab
- Straight-edge tool for cutting and making lines
- Craft glue
- Hot-glue gun
- Oven-proof plate
- Oven

Project Note

Refer to photo throughout.

Bunny & Eggs

1. Cut one section from ivory compound brick; cut off ¼ of section to use for bunny head, and reserve another ¼ for body. For head, soften compound, roll into ball, then shape into slight teardrop shape.

2. Referring to Fig. 1, push two seed beads on their sides into head for eyes; press until none of the bead hole shows. Using straight edge, indent two eyelashes for each eye.

Fig. 1

3. Roll pea-size ball of ivory compound; cut into eighths. Roll two of these small sections into tiny balls for bunny's "cheeks". Gently press side by side onto face.

4. Roll very tiny ball of dusty rose compound for nose; attach at top center between cheeks.

5. Roll pea-size ball of ivory compound; cut in half. Roll each half into ball; shape each into ½"-long cone for ear. Flatten cone slightly; round larger end. Apply pink blusher to center of ear with cotton-tip swab. Using straight edge, indent line down center of each ear. With pointed ends toward head, press ears together side by side; attach to head.

6. Roll ivory compound reserved in step 1 into a ball. Shape into slight teardrop shape for body.

7. Roll two pea-size balls of ivory compound for arms. Shape each into ½"-long cone; flatten and round larger end for paw. Attach smaller end to slightly pointed end of body.

8. Attach head on top of body and arms. Position arms on each side of head.

9. Roll marble-size balls of peach, turquoise and dusty rose compound; shape each into an egg.

10. Bake bunny and eggs on oven-proof plate in preheated 275-degree oven for 10 minutes. Cool completely.

Assembly

1. Wrap mauve ribbon around basket handle; secure with dots of hot glue. Tie two tiny bows of ribbon; glue one to each side where handle meets basket. Tie a third tiny bow and glue to bunny at base of ears.

2. Glue Easter grass in basket with craft glue. Hot-glue eggs onto grass, then hot-glue bunny behind eggs. Hold in place until glue cools.

Fluffy Lamb

These tiny sweeties are perfect for including in Easter baskets and scattering over your springtime table. Faces, ears and legs are quickly "sculpted," baked and glued to pompoms. Be daring—try pompoms in different springtime pastels!

Design by Jackie Haskell

Materials

- Black #042 Sculpey III modeling compound
- 2 black seed beads
- White pompoms: 1" and ¼"
- ⅛"-wide mauve satin ribbon
- Straight-edge tool for cutting and making lines
- Hot-glue gun
- Oven-proof plate
- Oven

Project Note

Refer to photo throughout.

Instructions

1. Roll six pea-size balls of modeling compound. Flatten and shape one into a teardrop shape with one end rounded and the other end pointed.

2. Referring to Fig. 1, push two seed beads on their sides into head for eyes; press until none of the bead hole shows. Using straight edge, indent two eyelashes for each eye. Roll very tiny ball of compound for nose; carefully press into place.

Fig. 1

3. Cut another of the pea-size balls into quarters. Mold one piece into a teardrop for ear; using straight edge, indent line down center of ear. Repeat to make second ear; attach ears at sides of head.

4. Roll each of the remaining pea-size balls into a leg—a round, thick column ½" long. Press legs together side by side in pairs; slightly flatten one end of each pair by pressing them carefully onto flat surface.

5. Bake head and leg pairs on oven-proof plate in preheated 275-degree oven for 10 minutes. Cool completely.

6. Glue head to 1" pompom. Trim one side of ¼" pompom to flatten it; glue flat side onto top of head.

Glue legs, flattened ends down, on bottom of 1" pompom.

7. Tie tiny bow of mauve ribbon; trim ends at an angle and glue to pompom below face. 🥚

Tiny Bunny Buddies

Imagine a whole Easter parade of these whimsical little bunnies marching up and down your holiday table! They're simple to create with precut wooden shapes.

Design by Vicki Blizzard

Materials

Each Bunny

- 1½"-tall wooden egg
- 2 (⁷⁄₁₆"-tall) wooden primitive hearts
- Ceramcoat acrylic paints from Delta Technical Coatings Inc.: Lisa pink #2084 White #2505
- Glossy water-base varnish from Delta Technical Coatings Inc.
- Paintbrushes: ½" paintbrush 1/0 liner brush
- ⅜" white pompom
- 6" piece (⅛"-wide) pastel satin ribbon
- Ice pick
- Crafter's Pick Ultimate Tacky Glue by API
- Black fine-line permanent marking pen
- Small craft saw

Project Notes

Refer to photo throughout.

Let glue, paint, ink and varnish dry between coats.

Instructions

1. Using ice pick, poke a small, deep hole in pointed end of egg. Glue point of one heart into hole with flat surface facing front.

2. For feet, saw a scant ¼" from tip of remaining heart. Glue broad end of egg to flat surface of heart toward back (sawed tip).

3. Using ½" brush, paint egg and hearts with two coats white paint. Using ½" brush or liner brush as desired, paint Lisa pink hearts for inner ears and bottoms of feet, small triangular nose and oval cheeks. Using liner brush and Lisa pink, dot four toes onto bottom of each foot.

4. Using marking pen throughout, draw dashed outline around and between pink ear centers and pink bottoms of feet; draw dashed line to define tops of feet; draw toes on tops and front edges of feet. Outline cheeks with dashed line; add nose, mouth, eyebrows and oval eyes.

5. Paint bunny with two coats varnish.

6. Glue pompom to back for tail. Tie ribbon in a bow; trim ends at an angle. Glue bow to front of rabbit.

Easter Chick Treat Jar

Filled with colorful jelly bird eggs or foil-wrapped chocolate eggs, this little jar is a sweet addition for any Easter basket. It can also be filled with yellow cellophane Easter grass and used as a table favor.

Design by Helen L. Rafson

Materials

- Small (3⅜"-tall) candy jar with screw-on lid from Provo Craft
- Yellow craft foam
- ½"-wide x ⅛"-thick wooden heart from Lara's Crafts
- Ceramcoat acrylic paints from Delta Technical Coatings Inc.:
  Tangerine #2043
  White #2505
  Black #2506
- 8½" piece rainbow-stripe ⅜"-wide ribbon
- Sponge
- Paintbrush
- Toothpick
- Black fine-line permanent marking pen
- Pinking shears or decorative-edge scissors
- Aleene's Thick Designer Tacky Glue from Duncan Enterprises

Project Note

Refer to photo throughout.

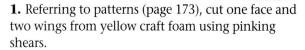

Instructions

1. Referring to patterns (page 173), cut one face and two wings from yellow craft foam using pinking shears.

2. Sponge tangerine paint around edges of face and wings, concentrating most of the paint on pinked edges with less paint toward center. Let dry. Repeat painting process on other sides of wings.

3. Glue face to jar lid; glue wings to sides of jar.

4. Dip end of paintbrush handle into black paint and dot two eyes onto chick's face; let dry. Dot on eye highlights with toothpick dipped in white paint; let dry. Draw eyelashes with marking pen.

5. For beak, paint all surfaces of heart with tangerine; let dry. Using marking pen, outline front surface of painted heart with tiny dashed line. Glue beak to face, point down.

6. Tie ribbon in bow; trim V-shaped notch in ribbon ends. Glue bow to bottom edge of face. Fill jar with treats.

Easter Basket Greeting Card

Send personalized springtime greetings with this colorful card. It boasts a whole clutch of colorful eggs cut from scraps of printed scrapbook papers.

Design by Kathy Wegner

Materials

- 6½" x 5" blank greeting card with envelope
- 5½" square brown kraft paper
- Assorted printed scrapbook papers
- Fiskars ripple-edge paper edgers #9204
- Mounting Memories Keepsake Glue from Beacon Adhesives
- Black fine-point permanent marking pen

Project Notes

Refer to photo throughout.

Read all package instructions before using Keepsake Glue.

Instructions

1. Referring to patterns (page 174), cut one basket from brown kraft paper using ripple-edge paper edgers. Using regular scissors, cut five eggs and one bow from assorted printed scrapbook papers.

2. Glue three eggs to card front; glue basket over eggs. Glue bow to basket handle and remaining eggs in front of basket.

3. Using marking pen, draw dashed outline around eggs; add dashed outline and other details to bow.

Blooming Beauties Frame

Mom would love to receive a photo of her little sweeties in this simple, colorful photo frame. It transforms even the plainest fridge into a work of art!

Design by Janna Britton

Materials

- Woodsies wooden cutouts from Forster Inc:
  2 large (1³⁄₁₆"-diameter) circles
  4 medium (¾"-diameter) circles
  6 medium (1⅛"-wide) hearts
  12 small (⅞"-wide) hearts
- 4 wooden craft sticks
- Americana acrylic paints from DecoArt:
  Kelly green #DA55
  Royal fuchsia #DA151
- ½" flat paintbrush
- Tulip pearl dimensional fabric paints from Duncan Enterprises:
  Pink pearl
  Sea mist pearl
- Aleene's Ultimate glue gun and low-temperature jewelry glue sticks from Duncan Enterprises
- Clear acrylic spray sealer
- 4 (1") sections of adhesive-backed magnet strip

Project Notes

Refer to photo throughout.

Let paints dry between coats.

Instructions

1. Mix equal parts kelly green paint and water. Paint all craft sticks and wooden hearts on tops and edges with mixture. Paint circles with undiluted royal fuchsia.

2. Glue craft sticks into a square frame.

3. Referring to patterns (page 174), arrange painted circles and hearts to make roses, with pointed ends of hearts forming points of leaves. Glue circles to hearts.

4. Glue one large rose in upper right corner of frame; glue a small rose on each side. Repeat with remaining roses in lower left corner.

5. Add swirls to rosebuds with pink pearl; add details to leaves with sea mist pearl.

6. Spray frame with clear acrylic sealer.

7. Attach a magnet section to back of frame at each corner. Tape or glue photo in frame. ❀

Succulent Strawberries

Nature's sweetest, most delectable springtime delights make a beautiful frame for a favorite snapshot. Precut wooden shapes are the key to quick and easy construction.

Design by Janna Britton

Materials

- Woodsies wooden cutouts from Forster Inc:
  4 large (1⅝"-wide) hearts
  4 medium (1⅛"-wide) hearts
  8 small (1³⁄₁₆"-wide) stars
- 4 wooden craft sticks
- Americana acrylic paints from DecoArt:
  Kelly green #DA55
  Santa red #DA170
- ½" flat paintbrush
- Tulip pearl dimensional fabric paints from Duncan Enterprises:
  Buttercup pearl
  Sea mist pearl
- Aleene's Ultimate glue gun and low-temperature jewelry glue sticks from Duncan Enterprises
- Clear acrylic spray sealer
- 4 (1") sections of adhesive-backed magnet strip
- Pliers

Project Notes

Refer to photo throughout.

Let paints dry between coats.

Instructions

1. Paint all hearts on tops and edges with Santa red. Holding star in hand with grain running across base of point(s), use pliers to snap one point off four stars and two points off remaining four stars. Paint stars on fronts and edges with kelly green.

2. Glue four-pointed stars to tops of large hearts and three-pointed stars to tops of medium hearts.

3. Glue craft sticks into a square frame. Glue one larger strawberry and one smaller strawberry to each corner, overlapping as desired.

4. Using sea mist pearl, paint details on strawberry tops. Using buttercup pearl, dot "seeds" onto red berries.

5. Spray frame with clear acrylic sealer.

6. Attach a magnet section to back of frame at each corner. Tape or glue photo in frame. ❀

Pierced Paper Creations

Decorative-edge scissors and a sharp needle are the keys to creating these delicate, lacy-looking Mother's Day tributes. The card is edged with real lace!

Designs by Helen L. Rafson

Materials

Both Projects

- Heavyweight art paper:
  8" x 6" piece for card
  2½" x 6¾" strip for bookmark
- Low-tack masking tape
- Tracing paper
- Foam-core board or other work surface
- Sharp needle
- Decorative-edge scissors
- Glue stick

Greeting Card

- Coordinating envelope at least 4⅜" x 6⅜"
- ¾" x 6" strip white lace

Bookmark

- 11" piece (⅛"-wide) pink satin ribbon
- Seam sealant
- Contact paper (optional)
- ¼" round hole punch

Project Notes

Refer to photo throughout.

Test masking tape on art paper to make sure it will not damage paper when it is peeled off. If needed, press tape onto your clothes and peel it off several times to make it less sticky.

Greeting Card

1. Fold 6" x 8" art paper in half to make 4" x 6" greeting card. Open card up again and lay it on foam-core board with inside of card facing board and card's front flap at bottom. Secure card with masking tape.

2. Measure and, using pencil, lightly mark center of card's front bottom edge. On right edge of card, lightly mark point ⅜" from bottom; repeat on left edge of card. Lightly draw straight line from each marked position on edge to marked center at bottom.

3. Trace pattern (page 175) onto tracing paper. Lay tracing paper over card, centering design on card front. Tape tracing paper in place.

4. With sharp needle, punch holes through tracing paper and card, following pattern lines and spacing holes evenly. Carefully remove tracing paper.

5. Carefully remove card from board. Using decorative-edge scissors, cut along pencil lines from side to bottom; erase any remaining pencil marks.

6. Apply glue to bottom ¾" on inside of card. Place lace over glue; let dry.

Bookmark

1. Trim edges of art paper with decorative-edge scissors. Tape bookmark to foam-core board.

2. Trace pattern (page 175) onto tracing paper. Lay tracing paper over bookmark, centering design. Tape tracing paper in place.

3. With sharp needle, punch holes through tracing paper and bookmark, following pattern lines and spacing holes evenly. Carefully remove tracing paper.

4. Carefully remove bookmark from board. If desired, seal bookmark between layers of clear contact paper at this point. Trim excess contact paper, leaving a margin of ⅛" on all sides.

5. Punch hole in center top of bookmark. Fold ribbon in half. Push loop through hole and draw ribbon ends through loop. Trim ribbon ends evenly. Treat cut edges with seam sealant; let dry. ❁

"Welcome, Little One"

Mother's Day is an extra-special occasion for expectant moms and those who have just welcomed a new baby. Both would love this charming gift featuring a stork created from precut wooden shapes. Personalize this fun design with a name and date, or paint baby's clothes or "sling" pink or blue, if you like.

Design by Kathy Wegner

Materials

- Wood products from Forster Inc.:
  2¾" x 7¼" wooden slat
  2 (3½") craft picks
- Woodsies wooden shapes from Forster Inc.:
  Large (2"-long) oval
  Medium (1½"-long) oval
  2 medium (1½"-long) teardrops
  Medium (¾"-diameter) circle
  Medium (1⁷⁄₁₆"-wide) triangle
- Aleene's Premium-Coat acrylic paints from Duncan Enterprises:
  Medium red #OC 102
  Medium orange #OC 114
  Medium yellow #OC 126
  White #OC 173
  Blush #OC 183
- 9" piece (⅜"-wide) white satin ribbon
- Black fine-line permanent marking pen
- Matte spray varnish
- Paintbrushes: ½" flat and one scruffy brush
- Thick tacky glue
- Waxed paper

Project Notes

Refer to photo throughout.

Pour small puddles of paint onto palette and thin each color with one or two drops of water before painting.

Matte spray varnish doesn't usually smear permanent black markers, but test yours to be sure.

Let all paints and ink dry before adding adjacent colors, ink details, glue or varnish.

Instructions

1. Paint wooden pieces on one side and edges: white—large oval (stork body), medium oval (baby body), one medium teardrop (wing) and head portion of remaining teardrop; medium orange—pointed section (beak area) on stork head and craft picks; blush—circle (baby head); medium yellow—triangle (baby's sling).

2. To blush baby's cheeks, dip dry scruffy brush into medium red; blot onto paper towel until almost no paint remains on brush. Lightly dab cheeks on baby's head until desired color is achieved.

3. With marking pen, add details: stork's eye, mouth and nostril, lines on wing; eyes on baby. Write "Welcome Little One!" at top of slat.

4. Referring to pattern, position stork pieces on slat and glue in place. With marker, draw lines from stork's mouth. Glue baby parts to slat.

5. Sandwich assembled plaque between layers of waxed paper; press plaque under heavy books until dry.

6. Spray completed plaque with matte varnish.

7. Glue ribbon ends to back of plaque for hanger. ❈

Father's Day Pencil Holder

This nautical desk accessory is a colorful reminder of the love and esteem that we feel for Dad all year-round! Let your youngster sponge-paint the can while you tackle the simple tin punch.

Design by Sandra Graham Smith

Materials

- 6" square aluminum flashing (see Project Notes)
- Empty 14½-ounce can, washed, dried, and with one end removed
- Enamel paints: red, white and blue
- Small paintbrush
- Small sponge
- Tracing paper
- Masking tape
- Hammer
- Several finishing nails
- Pressed-wood board or other hard, protective surface
- Tin snips
- 18" piece (⅛"-wide) white satin ribbon

Project Notes

Refer to photo throughout.

Remove or flatten any sharp edges around open end of can.

Let paint dry between coats and before applying adjacent colors.

Aluminum flashing is available at hardware stores.

Instructions

1. Place tracing paper over pattern (page 175); trace pattern.

2. Lay aluminum flashing on board; secure with masking tape. Lay traced pattern over aluminum; tape pattern to board so it will not shift.

3. Punch design with hammer and nail, moving from dot to dot and changing nail if point becomes dull. Punch holes in corners of boat so they will be large enough to tie ribbon through.

4. Remove pattern and tape. Using tin snips, cut out sailboat just outside punched lines. Turn punched aluminum over; rough side is right side of design.

5. Referring to photo, paint sailboat using thick strokes.

6. Sponge outside of can with white paint, then with red.

7. Tie sailboat to can, attaching ribbon through larger holes in corners of boat.

Nine Men's Morris Game

Dad will treasure this exquisite gift; it's as decorative as it is fun to play! Loaded with fishing motifs and crafted on a basswood plank with the bark still attached, it's a wonderful accent for cabin or lodge-style den! Be sure to include the playing instructions on the back of the game board.

Design by Sharon Tittle

Materials

- 11" x 13" bark preserved basswood plank #3510 from Walnut Hollow
- 2 wooden medallions #16302 from Walnut Hollow
- Ceramcoat acrylic paints from Delta Technical Coatings Inc.:
  Autumn brown #02055
  English yew green #02095
  Georgia clay #02097
  Bouquet pink #02132
  Misty mauve #02441
  Custard #02448
  Drizzle grey #02452
  Black cherry #02484
  White #02505
  Black #02506
  Calypso orange #02506
  Spring green #02517
  Dark goldenrod #02519
  Ocean mist blue #02529
  Silver pine #02534
- Stars & hearts #0476 Stencil Mini from from Delta Technical Coatings Inc.
- Robert Simmons Expressions paintbrushes:
  #0 script liner #E50
  #12 flat shader #E60
  #3 round #E85
- 9 (10mm) dark turquoise square beads from The Beadery
- 9 antique gold filigree beads from The Beadery
- 2 (1¼"-long) decorative fish beads
- Black fine-line permanent marking pen
- Matte-finish varnish from Delta Technical Coatings Inc.
- Graphite paper
- Towel or cloth
- Thick, white tacky glue
- Satin decoupage medium from Delta Technical Coatings Inc.

Project Notes

Refer to photo throughout.

Before transferring pattern to wood, study pattern (page 176) and note that in some areas, pattern is not to scale. Sketch basic lines of playing board first, then use pattern to accurately reproduce detailed areas like flies, lures and hooks.

Let all paints and ink dry before applying adjacent or overlaying colors, details, glue or varnish.

Instructions

1. Referring to pattern (page 176), transfer pattern to plank using graphite paper as needed and adjusting measurements as noted.

2. Using #0 script liner brush, stripe background of board and four corner squares using autumn brown. Shade squares on two sides in a solid coating of autumn brown. Shade outside of square lightly on two right sides in autumn brown to give dimension.

3. Thin one part custard paint with two parts water. Use this wash to paint center rectangle and outermost of three borders.

4. Thin silver pine paint in same manner and use wash to paint two borders between custard areas.

5. Paint medallions with a heavy coat of undiluted autumn brown; wipe off paint with cloth or towel, leaving more color in carved areas and less on flat surfaces. Center and glue medallions at top and bottom of board.

6. Paint fishing tackle according to pattern and color

key. Shade outside right edges of all pieces in a light hue of autumn brown and add highlights with white.

7. Outline everything with marking pen.

8. Coat the playing board and medallions with matte-finish varnish.

9. Type out or photocopy instructions (page 177); cut out and decoupage to back of playing board. Coat back of board with varnish.

10. Glue decorative fish beads to center custard rectangle. Use turquoise and gold beads for playing pieces. ✏

Playing instructions on page 177

Rockets' Red Glare Apron

You can start this apron on the morning of the Fourth, and wear it to flip burgers for your holiday cookout! Choose patriotic prints for the rockets and add "fuses" of seine twine.

Design by Nancy Marshall

Materials

- Off-white apron
- 6" x 9" piece red-and-white plaid fabric for rocket bodies
- 6" x 9" piece star-print blue fabric for rocket noses
- 2 (6" x 9") pieces HeatnBond Ultra Hold Iron-On Adhesive from Therm O Web
- 3 (2") pieces seine twine
- Iron

Project Note

Refer to photo throughout.

Instructions

1. Launder fabrics and apron without using fabric softener; iron as needed.

2. Following manufacturer's instructions, fuse adhesive to back of red and blue fabrics.

3. Referring to patterns (page 177), cut three rocket bodies from red fabric and three rocket noses from blue fabric.

4. Knot one end of each piece of twine.

5. Center rocket nose with top point 2" below top of apron; fuse. Center rocket body below fused nose; center one twine "fuse" at base of rocket, tucking unknotted end under fabric. Fuse rocket body in place.

6. Repeat with remaining rocket parts and twine, setting them at an angle as shown, or arranging them as desired. ★

Stars & Stripes Door Hanger

Just painting this bright holiday design will put you in a patriotic mood! Thanks to a ready-made door hanger, you don't need any carpenter skills to create a durable decoration you'll use year after year.

Design by Debbie Rines

Project Notes

Refer to photo throughout.

Let all paints and ink dry before adding adjacent colors, ink details, glue or finish.

Instructions

1. Using ¾" flat brush through step 4, apply primer to all wood pieces. Sand when dry.

2. Using white, paint door hanger, stars and one small craft stick.

3. With masking tape, tape off 1¼" stripe under hole. Using electric blue, paint taped-off area, large craft stick and one small craft stick.

4. Using true red, paint one small craft stick.

5. Following manufacturer's instructions, mix stencil medium and true red. Apply mixture to cosmetic sponge; pounce on paper towels first to remove most of paint. Then, using ¼" stripe on stencil, sponge mixture onto door hanger to make stripes below broad electric blue stripe.

6. Using marking pen throughout, print "Happy 4th of July" on large craft stick. Draw "stitching" lines around outside edge of door hanger, around hole, edges of stars, large craft stick and stripes. Add diagonal dashed lines to small craft sticks.

7. Thin white paint to consistency of ink. Using 10/0 liner brush, apply thinned mixture to left and bottom sides of lettering on large craft stick to highlight it. Using toothpick dipped in undiluted white, add dots to ends of letters.

8. Using ¾" flat brush, apply satin varnish to all wood pieces.

9. Using wire cutters, nip ends off painted small craft sticks so that they measure 3"–3¼" long. Curl one end of each piece of star garland.

10. Glue pieces together, gluing stars on electric blue stripe, and gluing cut ends of small craft stick "firecrackers" under large craft stick at base of hat. Glue straight end of star garland "fuse" under tip of each small craft stick. ★

Materials

- Wood products from Lara's Crafts:
  Adoorable door hanger #LAH 100
  3 (1") stars, ³⁄₁₆" thick
- 3 (2½") pieces gold metallic star garland
- One Heart … One Mind stencil #119
- ¾"-wide wooden craft stick
- 3 (³⁄₈"-wide) wooden craft sticks
- Aleene's Premium-Coat acrylic paints from Duncan Enterprises:
  True red #OC 103
  White #OC 173
  Electric blue #OC 218
- Aleene's All-Purpose Primer #EN 104 from Duncan Enterprises
- Aleene's Stencil Medium #EN 115 from Duncan Enterprises
- Aleene's Satin Varnish #EN 102 from Duncan Enterprises
- Aleene's Thick Designer Tacky Glue from Duncan Enterprises
- Paintbrushes:
  ¾" flat
  10/0 liner
- Cosmetic sponge
- Black fine-line permanent marking pen
- Wire cutters
- Masking tape
- Toothpick
- Sandpaper

Patriotic Memo Holder

Uncle Sam left his top hat behind—and now it will hold your favorite memo pad or message on your refrigerator or any other metal surface. The tin punch is quick, and the painting is easy and bold!

Design by Sandra Graham Smith

Materials

- 9" square aluminum flashing (see Project Notes)
- Enamel paints: red, white, yellow and blue
- Small paintbrush
- Tracing paper
- Masking tape
- Hammer
- Several finishing nails
- Pressed-wood board or other hard, protective surface
- Tin snips
- Wooden spring-type clothespin
- 2½" piece of ½"-wide adhesive-backed magnet
- Memo pad
- Hot-glue gun

Aluminum flashing is available at hardware stores.

Instructions

1. Place tracing paper over pattern (page 178); trace pattern.

2. Lay aluminum flashing on board; secure with masking tape. Lay traced pattern over aluminum; tape pattern to board so it will not shift.

3. Punch design with hammer and nail, moving from dot to dot and changing nail if point becomes dull.

4. Remove pattern and tape. Using tin snips, cut out hat just outside punched lines. Turn punched aluminum over; rough side is right side of design.

5. Referring to photo, paint hat using thick strokes.

6. Press magnet strip onto one flat surface of clothespin. Hot-glue painted tin hat to other flat side of clothespin. Insert memo pad in jaws of clothespin. ★

Project Notes

Refer to photo throughout.

Let paint dry between coats and before applying adjacent colors.

Pumpkin Pals Magnet

This black kitty-cat and smiling jack-o'-lantern are cute as can be, and would love to spend the Halloween holiday on your fridge door!

Design by Jackie Haskell

Fig. 1

Materials

- Sculpey III modeling compound:
  Sweet potato #033
  Black #042
  Dusty rose #303
  Emerald #323
- 4 (3mm) black ball beads
- ½" button magnet or magnet strip
- Pink powdered cosmetic blusher
- Cotton-tip swab
- Straight-edge tool for cutting and making lines
- Round wooden toothpick
- Straight pin
- Craft glue
- Oven-proof plate
- Oven

Fig. 2

Jack-o'-Lantern

1. Cut one section from sweet potato compound brick and use ½ of this section. Soften compound, roll into ball, then shape into slight teardrop, with one end wider than the other.

2. Referring to Fig. 1, push two ball beads into head for eyes; roll small ball of sweet potato compound and attach for nose.

3. Apply pink blusher to cheeks with cotton-tip swab. Using straight pin, make lines for eyelashes, eyebrows and mouth.

4. Using toothpick, make hole in top center of jack-o'-lantern for stem. Starting at this hole, use straight edge to make lines down pumpkin forehead and from mouth to bottom of chin.

5. Cut a pea-size ball of emerald compound in half; roll this small piece into a ball, then roll into a 1½"-long rope. Stick one end into hole in top of jack-o'-lantern, then twist the remainder like a vine and attach to side of pumpkin.

6. Roll other half of emerald ball into a small ball, then form ball into a cone. Stick point into hole in top of jack-o'-lantern for stem; bend stem over slightly.

Black Cat

1. Cut one section from black compound brick and use ¼ of this section for cat's head. Soften compound, roll into ball, then shape into slight teardrop.

2. Referring to Fig. 2, push two ball beads into head for eyes; use straight pin for eyelashes and eyebrows.

3. Roll a pea-size ball of black compound; cut into quarters. Roll two of these pieces into small balls; press to cat's face for cheeks. Roll a tiny, tiny ball of dusty rose compound and affix atop cheeks for nose.

4. Use remaining quarters of pea-size ball for ears. Roll each into a ball, then shape into a teardrop with pointed end. Make lines down centers of ears with straight edge and attach to cat's head.

5. Roll a pea-size ball of black compound for each arm. Roll each piece into a ¾"-long cone; check fatter ends to make sure they are the same size. Flatten thicker ends slightly and shape into paws. Attach smaller ends of arms under back of head.

6. Carefully press head and arms onto pumpkin; use straight edge to define toes on paws.

7. Roll pea-size ball of black compound into ¾"-long cone for tail. Flatten one end slightly and attach other end to back of jack-o'-lantern by cat's head, curling out slightly.

Finishing

1. Bake figure on oven-proof plate in preheated 275-degree oven for 10 minutes. Cool completely.

2. Glue magnet to back of baked figure.

Sammy Scarecrow Hanging

Revel in the warm hues of autumn with this fun painting project! Our sample is painted on heavy brown kraft paper, but you could also recreate the design on ¾" pine. Don't get hung up on positioning every spot of color, every line of detail. Just relax—and have fun! We promise you'll love the results!

Design by Doxie Keller for DecoArt

Materials

- 1 yard (30"-wide) heavy kraft paper
- Americana acrylic paints from DecoArt:
  Titanium white #DA01
  Tangerine #DA12
  Mistletoe #DA53
  Dark chocolate #DA65
  Lamp black #DA67
  Base flesh #DA136
  Primary red #DA199
  Primary blue #DA200
  Primary yellow #DA201
- Loew-Cornell paintbrushes:
  801 liner #1
  #8, ¾" and #4 Series 7300 flat shaders
  Spatter brush
- Polyester fiberfill
- Tan embroidery floss and large-eye needle
- 34" 18- to 20-gauge wire
- Wire cutters
- Several strips of torn fabric
- Hot-glue gun
- Photocopier with enlarging capability
- Pinking Shears

Project Notes

Refer to photo throughout.

Use whichever painting methods you prefer. On sample, highlights and shading were generally added while initial application of paint was still wet. Float shades and highlights if you prefer. Experiment with mixing colors and using different brushes to achieve different effects.

Painting

1. Referring to patterns (page 178 and 179), enlarge scarecrow and "BOO!" sign to 167 percent; lightly sketch pattern, including outline, on 16" x 12" piece kraft paper. Reproduce "BOO!" portion on a 13" x 4" piece kraft paper.

2. Use tangerine to paint "BOO!"; add tangerine wavy lines at ends as shown. Highlight letters on left sides with titanium white. Outline letters with lamp black.

3. Hat is a float of primary yellow with tangerine shading on hatband.

4. Paint jacket tangerine. Highlight front placket and folds with primary yellow. Paint collar mistletoe using dark chocolate for shadowed underside. Paint straw coming from sleeves, pocket, shirt front and hat with primary yellow highlighted with titanium white and outlined with lamp black.

5. Patches may be primary red, primary blue or mistletoe with stripes or contrasting polka dots. Paint belt, neck ribbon and shadow under right side of jacket with primary red; shade and outline with lamp black. Highlight belt and ribbon with white.

6. Pants are floats of dulled blue. Post is dark chocolate; highlight corner with titanium white.

7. Use base flesh on face, filling in cheeks and mouth with primary red; shade nose lightly with primary red.

8. Paint bird with primary blue, adding highlights with touches of titanium white and shading with touches of lamp black.

9. Go over design to restore any lost outlines with liner brush and ebony black.

10. Using spatter brush, spatter painted designs very lightly with ebony black and titanium white paints.

Assembly

1. Cut matching pieces of paper for backs of scarecrow and "BOO!" pieces. Sew fronts and backs together with running stitches sewn with four strands embroidery floss, making an oval-shaped frame around scarecrow and a slightly curved oval around "BOO!" as in photo. As you sew, insert some stuffing between pieces to give hanging a slightly puffy dimension. Trim edges ½" around stitching with pinking shears.

2. Cut two 8" pieces wire; use to suspend scarecrow from "BOO!," curling excess wire ends. Tie a couple torn fabric strips in knot around one of the hanging wires.

3. Form remaining 18" piece of wire into hanging loop, inserting ends through top of "BOO!" sign and curling excess wire ends.

4. Knot a few more torn fabric strips; hot-glue to bottom right of scarecrow sign.

Candy Cane Cats

With all the beautiful colors and delectable flavors of "designer" candy canes available,
it's a shame to enjoy them only at Christmastime! These clever kittens make
wonderful treats for the little "tricksters" who'll be ringing your doorbell on Halloween.

Designs by Heather Bell Henry

Materials

- Rainbow Felt Classics by Kunin Felt:
  5" square gold #352
  2" square French vanilla #395
  5" square white #550
  5" square black #937
- 6 (⅜") white or clear buttons
- 9 (2") pieces silver Misuhiki cord #1083-21 by Darice
- 19 x 10.5mm holly leaves from The Beadery:
  2 emerald #007
  2 ruby #017
  2 topaz #025
- So-Soft Dimensional paints from DecoArt:
  Christmas red #DD105
  Christmas green #DD112
  Black #DD112
  Gold glitter #DD303
- Candy canes: 1 each butterscotch, licorice and peppermint, or desired flavors
- Tacky craft glue

Butterscotch

1. Referring to patterns on facing page, cut one body and one ear strip from gold felt; referring to photo, cut eight stripes from French vanilla felt. Carefully cut slits on body for ears.

2. Glue one stripe at center tip of each end of ear; let dry. Fold ear piece lengthwise; insert ends through slits from back.

3. Glue two buttons to face for eyes, filling button holes with glue. For wiskers, center three 2" pieces silver Misuhiki cord, separating ends slightly; glue at center with small dot of craft glue. Let dry.

4. Using photo as a guide, paint center of each eye with Christmas green dimensional paint; paint collar with alternating dots of Christmas green and gold glitter dimensional paints. Glue topaz holly leaves below collar; dot tip of each leaf with gold glitter paint.

5. Using black dimensional paint, paint iris in center of green circle on eyes; paint over glue at center of whiskers for nose. Add small dot of Christmas red paint below nose for tongue.

6. Glue three stripes on each side of body; let dry. Slip center part of ears behind head over straight end of candy cane with curved end over front of cat for tail.

Licorice

1. Referring to patterns, cut one body and one ear strip from black felt; cut two Licorice inner ears from white felt. Carefully cut slits on body for ears.

2. Glue inner ear at each end of ear; let dry. Fold ear piece lengthwise; insert ends through slits from back.

3. Repeat step 3 of Butterscotch.

4. Using photo as a guide, paint center of each eye with Christmas green dimensional paint; paint collar with alternating dots of Christmas red and gold glitter dimensional paints. Glue emerald holly leaves below collar; dot tip of each leaf with gold glitter paint.

5. Using black dimensional paint, paint iris in center of green circle on eyes; paint over glue at center of whiskers for nose. Add small dot of Christmas red paint below nose for tongue.

6. Slip center part of ears behind head over straight end of candy cane with curved end over front of cat for tail.

Peppermint

1. Referring to patterns, cut one body and one ear strip from white felt. Carefully cut slits on body for ears.

2. Fold ear piece lengthwise; insert ends through slits from back.

3. Repeat step 3 of Butterscotch.

4. Repeat steps 4–6 of Licorice, substituting ruby holly leaves for emerald.

Body
Cut 3 from felt

Slit

Slit

Fold Line

Ear
Cut 3 from felt

Butterscotch Inner Ear
Cut 2 from French vanilla felt

Licorice Inner Ear
Cut 2 from white felt

Butterscotch Stripe
Cut 8 from French vanilla fe

Friendly Fall Scarecrow

This friendly fellow will bring a smile to everyone who sees him. He's purposely constructed so as to be flat enough to hang happily between your storm door and front door. And because he's naturally "hinged," he's easy to fold up and store in a large plastic bag until next autumn.

Design by Florence Bolen Tebbets

Materials
- 5-foot glow-in-the-dark skeleton
- Small- or medium-size recycled flannel shirt
- Child's or adult small-size recycled blue jeans
- 1 pair canvas or gardening gloves
- 1 pair recycled socks
- 24" square burlap in color of your choice
- 3 yards natural jute twine
- ½ yard muslin
- 1 yard polyester quilt batting
- Polyester fiberfill
- 8–10 light tan chenille stems
- 1 skein soft sand Aleene's Satin Sheen Twisted Ribbon by Duncan Enterprises
- Assorted fabric scraps
- Assorted embellishments: sunflowers, small stuffed crow, fall leaves, enamel apples, ornament corn, pumpkins, small pinecones, berries, etc.
- Thick craft glue or low-temperature glue gun
- Black marking pen
- Acrylic paints: black and white
- Small flat paintbrush
- Powdered cosmetic blusher

Project Note
Refer to photo throughout for placement and facial details.

Head

1. To make hanger, cut ½-yard piece of jute twine; loop through hole in top of skeleton's head and knot.

Work around hanger while attaching hat. (Or, add hanger around scarecrow's neck after he is assembled.)

2. Cut quilt batting in half; set one piece aside. Keeping back of head fairly flat, wrap batting around skeleton's head, rounding face as much as possible. Leave opening at neck edge. Through neck opening, stuff several handfuls of loose polyester fiberfill under batting to make a nicely rounded face.

3. Fold muslin in half; cut small slit in center on fold. Slip muslin over batting and pull hanger through slit. Smooth muslin over batting on back of head and glue to neck edge if necessary. Smooth muslin over face. Glue side edges to back of head. Gather bottom edges of muslin around neck; secure with chenille stem.

Clothes

1. Dress scarecrow in jeans. Secure jeans to rib cage by looping chenille stem through a belt loop; wrap stem around rib and back through belt loop. Repeat with each belt loop.

2. Dress scarecrow in shirt; button closed. Tie remaining jute around waist for belt; knot each end.

Feet & Hands

1. For feet, cut reserved batting into four strips. Wrap two around one foot and ankle, padding toes and foot well. Pull sock on over batting. Secure sock to leg bone with chenille stem. Repeat with remaining foot.

2. For hands, lightly stuff each finger of gloves with fiberfill. Slip glove over each hand, working fingers into glove. Lightly fill gloves with loose fiberfill to round them out nicely. Secure gloves to wrist bones with chenille stems.

Hat

1. Tear 4"-wide strip of fabric to tie bow at top of hat; set aside.

2. Fold burlap in half diagonally; cut on fold. Reserve one piece for another use. Place longer cut side of remaining burlap triangle around scarecrow's head, bringing raw edges to back of head; glue in place.

3. Adjust top of hat to scarecrow's head. Fold back edge for brim, if desired. Gather top of hat into a peak. Tie bow around it with fabric strip.

Hair

1. From twisted ribbon, cut four 12" pieces and two 10" pieces. Untwist each by holding both ends and twisting in opposite directions. Fan ribbon out flat, leaving 1" of one end on each piece tightly twisted.

2. From flat end, tear ribbon along its length into thin strands up to the point where it is still twisted.

3. Applying glue to twisted ends, glue two 12" pieces and one 10" piece on each side of scarecrow's face. Tuck glued ends up under hat, staggering lengths of straw pieces.

4. From remaining twisted ribbon, cut two 6" pieces. Untwist and tear as in steps 1 and 2.

5. Remove a small strip from each piece; gather the rest of the strips and tie a knot around center of each strip. Fold pieces in half; glue knots under hat for bangs.

6. From remaining twisted ribbon, cut three 8" pieces. Set one piece aside for neck; untwist other two as instructed in steps 1 and 2.

7. Remove small strip from each piece; gather the rest of the strips and tie a knot around the center of each strip. Fold pieces in half; glue knots over tops of gloves under shirt cuffs. Curl some of the ribbon over a scissors blade as you would curling ribbon, if desired.

Finishing

1. Test marking pen in an inconspicuous spot to make sure it does not bleed on fabric. Using marking pen, draw face on scarecrow; add stitch lines around nose and along mouth.

2. Apply blush to cheeks and nose.

3. Using black acrylic paint, paint pupils of eyes. When dry, paint whites of eyes with white acrylic paint, and add white highlight dot to pupils using end of paintbrush handle or toothpick.

4. Tear 4"-wide strip of fabric for bow tie; tie around neck under collar, adjusting fullness as necessary. Tie into a bow.

5. Unwind and fray remaining 8" strip of ribbon as for straw; glue under collar to frame face.

6. Glue assorted patches of fabric to hat, shirt and jeans. Add sunflower or package of seeds to his pocket. Embellish hat as desired.

Optional Variations

Consider the following options for your scarecrow:

1. Glue small stuffed crow or bird and bird nest to hat.

2. Tuck into his pocket a small wooden sign which has been printed with a message like "No Crows Allowed," "Crow Crossing," "Bountiful Harvest," etc.

3. Embellish scarecrow with assorted small gourds, miniature pumpkins, ornamental corn, pinecones, etc.

4. Substitute shredded corn husks for ribbon when making hair.

5. Dress scarecrow in a cast-off fedora or other man's hat and necktie.

Broom Buddy

This wonderful character will add a delightful touch to your door, porch
or entryway. He's easy and quick to construct using a ready-made broom.

Design by Florence Bolen Tebbets

Materials

- 36" straw broom
- 2 (35mm) wiggle eyes
- 2 (9" x 12") pieces orange felt
- Felt scraps: tan, dark brown, pink and hunter green
- 2 dark brown chenille stems
- ¼ yard fabric in an autumn print
- Assorted fabric scraps
- Lady bug
- Polyester fiberfill
- Thick craft glue or low-temperature glue gun
- Shiny black dimensional craft paint
- Black marking pen
- Powdered cosmetic blusher

Project Note

Refer to photo throughout for placement and facial details.

Instructions

1. Make hanging loop from one chenille stem. Secure on back of broom.

2. For headband, cut 3"-wide strip from the length of the autumn print fabric. Fold raw edges toward center. Beginning at back, glue headband around top portion of broom. Trim excess, reserving scraps.

3. Using one 35mm wiggle eye as a pattern, draw two circles on pink felt; cut out. Cut also a small pink triangle for nose.

4. For eyelids, cut one 2½"-diameter circle from tan felt; cut circle in half. Glue one half-circle to top of each eye so edges extend over edges of eye.

5. Spread glue on backs of eyes and on edges of eyelids; press into place on broom. Glue nose and cheeks in place.

6. Test marking pen in an inconspicuous spot to make sure it does not bleed on felt. Using marking pen, add stitch lines around nose and cheeks. Brush cheeks and nose with powdered blush.

7. For bow, tear 4"-wide strip from the length of the autumn print fabric; tie in bow around neck. Tie small strips of scrap fabrics around small strands of "hair" at top of broom. Tear a small fabric strip; tie in a bow and glue to headband. If desired, add a sunflower or other fall novelty.

8. Round off corners of one 9" x 12" piece orange felt to make pumpkin shape. Make small rounded cut in center top and bottom.

9. Working with a small section at a time, run a bead of glue around edge of pumpkin shape and glue to remaining orange felt, leaving small opening at top for stuffing. Trim excess fabric from second piece of felt to match top pumpkin. Using black marking pen, draw some lines down front of pumpkin. Stuff pumpkin very lightly with fiberfill.

10. Cut a small curved stem from dark brown felt; glue stem in top opening of pumpkin and glue pumpkin closed.

11. From hunter green felt, cut leaf. Add veins with black marking pen. Glue leaf to front of pumpkin at stem.

12. Glue pumpkin to front of broom. Further secure pumpkin by wrapping brown chenille stem around broom handle over brown felt stem. Twist tightly with stem ends in front. Curl ends around pencil; slide off to leave tendrils at front of pumpkin.

13. Glue ladybug onto leaf.

14. Paint a smile with shiny black dimensional paint; set aside to dry thoroughly. ***Hint:*** *To get an even smile, make one small dot on each cheek, then connect dots with paint.*

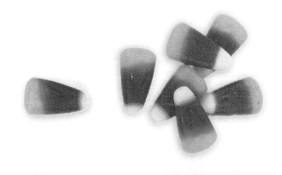

Spooky Magnet Trio

These fun Halloween characters are a snap to make from craft foam.
They'd also make wonderful decorations for your haunted house party!

Designs by Kathy Wegner

Materials

- Craft foam:
  4½" x 6" white
  3½" x 6½" black
  3½" x 5" orange
- Scribbles 3-D paints from Duncan Enterprises:
  Shiny lime green #SC164
  Shiny bright yellow #SC112
- Tulip slick paints from Duncan Enterprises:
  Black #65038
  Orange #65131
- 6¾"-length garland of 13mm plastic pumpkins
- Black fine-line permanent marking pen
- 3 (4") sections (½"-wide) adhesive-backed magnet
- Thick tacky glue
- Needle

Project Note

Refer to photo throughout.

Instructions

1. Referring to patterns (page 180), cut ghost from white craft foam, bat from black craft foam and jack-o'-lantern from orange craft foam.

2. Add painted details as follows:

Orange—cheeks and hearts.

Shiny lime green—jack-o'-lantern stem and bat eyes.

Shiny bright yellow—jack-o'-lantern nose and bat's mouth.

Black—eyes on ghost, eyes and mouth on jack-o'-lantern, and pupils in bat's shiny lime green eyes.

3. Using marking pen, draw dashed line around edges of jack-o'-lantern and ghost and their hearts; add smile to ghost and eyebrows to both characters.

4. Using needle, thread ends of pumpkin garland through ghost's hands; knot on wrong side to secure.

5. Affix magnet to back of each foam shape.

Autumn Leaves

There's nothing like the colors of fall—rich hues of burgundy, gold, orange, brown and yellow, creating a warm patchwork all around us! Bring the season's colors to your table on linens boasting appliqués cut from fall print fabrics.

Designs by Deborah S. Brooks

Materials

Each Place Mat & Napkin

- 1 yard three-layer quilted muslin from The Warm Company
- 18½" square muslin
- 4 yards matching triple-fold bias tape
- Thread to match muslin
- 1 yard fall leaves fabric from Cranston Creative Fabrics
- Fusible web
- Gold glitter dimensional fabric paint
- Iron
- Sewing machine

Project Note

Refer to photo throughout.

Place Mat

1. Trace 19" x 14" oval outline onto paper side of fusible web; cut identical oval from quilted muslin.

2. Following manufacturer's instructions, fuse web to

Continued on page 132

wrong side of fall leaves fabric. Trim out center area in one piece, leaving leaves along edges for detail. (Reserve cut-out leaves for napkin.) Cut out leaf frame along oval outline; fuse fabric to right side of muslin place mat.

3. Apply bias tape around edges of place mat.

4. Highlight leaves with gold glitter fabric paint as desired.

Napkin

1. Press under ¼" hem all around muslin square. Press under another ½" hem, mitering corners. Stitch around edges by hand or machine.

2. From leaves fabric reserved from center of place

mat, cut a section with 90-degree corner to fit in one corner of napkin. Trim away excess, detailing leaves on one side.

3. Remove paper backing. Following manufacturer's instructions, fuse fabric to right side of napkin.

4. Highlight leaves with gold glitter fabric paint as desired.

Fall Splendor Place Settings

Adorn your table with seasonal beauty when you set it with these dishes kissed with autumn gold. They go beautifully with the Autumn Leaves linens on page 131.

Designs by Deborah S. Brooks

Materials

Each Place Setting

- 7" glass plate
- 9" glass plate
- 12" wooden charger
- Gold Leaf Rub 'n Buff by Amaco
- Etch All etching creme
- Etch All Tip Kit
- 18-karat Gold Leafing Pen from Krylon
- Burnt orange acrylic paint
- Paintbrush
- Felt-tip pen
- Masking tape
- Glossy sealant

Project Notes

Carefully read instructions for etching products and rub-on gold leaf before beginning.

Wooden charger is for decorative use only.

Refer to photo throughout.

7" Plate

1. Referring to patterns (page 181), tape pattern for leaf cluster facedown on right side of glass plate, centering it carefully. Turn plate over so wrong side is facing you.

2. Trace pattern on wrong side of plate with felt-tip pen. Remove pattern.

3. Following manufacturer's instructions, trace pattern again on back of plate using etching crème and tip kit. Rinse and dry as directed.

4. Following manufacturer's instructions, apply rub-on gold leaf to etched design.

9" Plate

Follow instructions for 7" plate, substituting leaf border pattern and applying it around rim of plate.

Charger

1. Paint wooden plate on all surfaces with burnt orange paint, adding a second coat if necessary. Let dry.

2. Following manufacturer's instructions, apply gold leafing pen along outer edge. Let dry.

3. Spray plate with glossy sealant.

The Night Before Christmas

Need a quick gift to finish up your holiday gift list? This chapter brings you more than a dozen great ideas for spreading holiday cheer!

Felt Snowman & Santa

From start to finish, you can create this happy snowman or cheery Santa Claus in an hour or less!

Designs by Kathy Wegner

Materials

Snowman

- 9" x 12" white Rainbow Plush felt from Kunin Felt
- Rainbow Felt from Kunin Felt:
  1" x 1½" orange
  1½" x 3½" blueberry bash
  ½" x 10½" pirate green
- 7 (5mm) black round half-beads
- 3" (¼"-wide) black ribbon
- 2 (½") red pompoms
- 2 (3") natural-color Paper Capers paper-covered wires
- Ice pick or pointed stick

Santa

- Rainbow Felt from Kunin Felt:
  9" x 12" ruby
  1½" x 2" teal
  1½" square apricot
  2" x 2½" cashmere tan
- 4" square white Rainbow Plush felt from Kunin Felt
- 2 black seed beads

Each Design

- 6" x 2¹⁵⁄₁₆" plastic foam cone
- Thick tacky glue

Project Note

Refer to photo throughout for placement.

Snowman

1. Referring to patterns, enlarging body 105 percent (page 182), cut one body from white plush felt, one snowman nose from orange, and four mittens from blueberry bash.

2. Glue bottom of cone to a leftover piece of white plush felt; let dry. When glue is dry, trim off excess felt. Fringe ends of pirate green felt strip to make scarf.

Form nose by rolling side A of orange nose toward side B into a cone shape; secure with glue.

3. Glue white plush body to cone, letting excess stick up at top. Let glue dry. Using a pencil, push a hole in top of cone; fill hole with glue and push excess felt into hole with pencil.

4. To front of snowman (seamless side), glue two half-beads for eyes and five for mouth; glue base of orange cone nose to face. Glue scarf around neck, crossing ends in front.

5. Glue ends of black ribbon to sides of head for earmuffs band; ribbon should stand up off top of head a bit. Add red pompom on each side for earmuffs, concealing ribbon ends.

6. Sandwich one end of each piece of paper wire between two mittens; glue. With ice pick or pointed stick, poke a hole in each side of snowman; apply glue to paper wire ends of arms and insert one into each hole, pushing it in a bit. Let dry.

Santa

1. Referring to patterns (page 182), cut one body from ruby felt, one beard, one mustache and two cuffs from white plush, one sack from cashmere tan, two mittens from teal and one face from apricot.

2. Glue a leftover piece of ruby felt to bottom of cone; let dry. When glue is dry, trim off excess felt.

3. Glue ruby body to cone, letting excess stick up at top. Let glue dry. Using a pencil, push a hole in top of cone; fill hole with glue and push excess felt into hole with pencil.

4. To front of Santa (seamless side), glue beard, then face and mustache. Glue seed beads for eyes. Add sack, then mittens, then cuffs. ●

"We Believe in Angels"

This sweet design works up quickly with the help of wooden cutouts.

Design by Kathy Wegner

Materials

- 2¾" x 7¼" wooden slat from Forster Inc.
- Woodsies wooden cutout shapes from Forster Inc.:
  4 medium (1½") triangles
  3 small (⅞") stars
  2 medium (¾"-diameter) circles
  2 large (2") teardrops
- Aleene's Premium-Coat Acrylics paints from Duncan Enterprises:
  Medium red #OC 102
  Deep blue #OC 152
  White #OC 173
  Blush #OC 183
  Gold #OC 301
  Silver #OC 303
- Scribbles 3-D paints from Duncan Enterprises:
  Glittering gold #SC 302
  Glittering silver #SC 305
- 3-D Paint Matte Sealer #SP 508 from Duncan Enterprises
- Sponge brush (optional)
- Paintbrushes: flat, liner and scruffy
- Thick tacky glue
- 9" gold elastic cord
- Black fine-point permanent marking pen
- Palette or plastic foam plate
- Paper towels
- Waxed paper
- Craft drill with ⅛" bit

Project Notes

Refer to photo throughout.

Test to be sure matte sealer doesn't smear your black marking pen.

Squeeze a small puddle of paint onto palette and mix with one or two drops of water; use this mixture for all painting except base-coating slat.

Except for slat, paint wooden pieces on edges and one side only.

Let all paints dry between coats and before applying inked details.

Instructions

1. Drill hole through two top corners of slat.

2. Mix quarter-size puddle of deep blue paint with 1 tablespoon water. Using this wash and sponge or flat brush, base-coat slat on all surfaces.

3. Paint wooden cutouts as follows: white—all triangles; blush—both circles; silver acrylic—both teardrops; gold acrylic—all stars.

4. Using liner brush and undiluted white paint, paint "We believe in angels" diagonally across center of plaque.

5. Dry-brush cheeks onto angel heads: Dip scruffy brush into medium red; blot off excess onto paper towels until almost no paint remains on brush. Dab cheeks lightly with dry brush. Repeat as necessary.

6. Using marking pen, dot tiny eyes onto angel heads; draw feather details on white painted triangles (wings).

7. Glue painted wooden parts to slat as shown. Sandwich plaque between sheets of waxed paper and weight down with large book to hold flat until dry.

8. Highlight stars and add dots to background with gold

Continued on page 184

Festive Gift Bags

Give those special gifts in special wrappings: colorful gift bags decorated with holiday designs. Our examples have a decidedly country flair, but you can adapt the method and materials to suit your own tastes.

Designs by Mary Ayres

M a t e r i a l s

Each Gift Bag

- 7¾" x 9¾" natural kraft gift bag from Santa's Workbench
- Wonder Under fusible transfer webbing from Pellon
- 3 assorted buttons
- Stencil sheeting and craft knife
- Stencil brush
- Tacky craft glue
- Medium-point black marking pen
- Iron

Snowman

- Homespun fabric scraps in assorted small plaids, checks, stripes or prints: off-white/ecru, black, orange and 3 assorted prints
- Hunter green and country red stencil paint
- Brown Americana acrylic paint from DecoArt
- Small all-purpose paintbrush

Christmas Tree

- Homespun fabric scraps in assorted small plaids, checks, stripes or prints: green, brown, gold and 3 assorted prints
- Country red stencil paint

P r o j e c t   N o t e s

Let paints dry thoroughly between coats and before fusing fabric in place.

Refer to photo throughout for placement.

I n s t r u c t i o n s

1. Referring to checkerboard pattern (page 184), cut checkerboard stencil from stencil sheeting using craft knife. Using stencil brush, stencil gift bag using hunter green for snowman bag, and country red for Christmas tree bag.

2. Following manufacturer's instructions throughout, fuse transfer webbing onto wrong side of fabrics. Referring to patterns (pages 139 and 183), trace pieces onto fabrics:

Snowman Bag: snowman—off-white; hat—black; carrot nose—orange; hat and patches—remaining assorted prints.

Christmas Tree Bag: tree trunk—brown; star—gold; tree—green; patches—remaining assorted prints.

Cut out. Position fabric pieces in place and fuse; let cool.

3. Using medium-point marking pen, outline each fabric piece.

4. Glue button to center of each patch.

Finishing Snowman

1. Using black marking pen, draw dots for snowman eyes, mouth and buttons, as shown on pattern.

2. Dip stencil brush in country red paint; wipe excess on a paper towel until brush is almost completely dry with no brush strokes showing. Rub brush across snowman cheeks in circular motion.

3. Using medium-point marking pen, draw snowman arms on front of bag; paint with brown acrylic paint.

Snowman

Golden Poinsettia Angels

Imagine a whole "flock" of these angelic ornaments hanging from your tree, or dangling from an evergreen garland. Leaves from a silk poinsettia give them their glitter!

Design by Carol Dace

Materials

Each Angel

- 1"-diameter plastic foam ball
- 2"-diameter plastic foam ball
- 4"-diameter gold silk poinsettia blossom
- 6"-diameter gold silk poinsettia blossom
- 1" square pink felt
- 12" (3"-wide) sheer gold wire-edge ribbon
- Bumples textured yarn from One & Only Creations
- Ultra-fine-point black permanent marking pen
- 1 yard (¼"-wide) metallic gold woven ribbon
- 14mm gold bell or charm
- Powdered cosmetic blusher
- 8" monofilament fish line or thread
- 4" square cardboard
- Quarter
- Floral Pro glue gun with needle nozzle and Crafty Magic Melt glue sticks from Adhesive Technologies Inc.
- Small paintbrush
- Toothpick
- 4 straight pins
- Sharpened pencil
- Wire cutter

Project Note

Refer to photo throughout.

Instructions

1. Take poinsettias apart; remove plastic veins.

2. Cut wire-edge ribbon into 5" and 7" pieces. Pull wire along one edge of 7" piece to gather ribbon tightly; twist wire ends to secure. For body, enclose 2" plastic foam ball inside gathered ribbon and pull wire on other edge of ribbon to gather ribbon around ball; twist wire ends to secure. Clip off wire ends and save them.

3. Place a dab of glue in center of gathers; push toothpick through glue into center of ball, inserting about three-quarters of toothpick. Place large circle of poinsettia petals over toothpick, then small circle of poinsettia petals. Secure with glue without gluing down ends of petals.

4. For arms, cut 5" piece of ribbon in half lengthwise to make two 1½" x 5" pieces. Gather middle of one piece; secure gathers and attach bell using reserved piece of wire. Gather each end of ribbon; fasten with wire. Pin each end to body behind toothpick at ribbon seam, making both arms with this piece.

5. For face, using quarter as template, trace circle onto wrong side of pink felt; cut out. Glue felt circle to 1" plastic foam ball.

6. For hair, wrap yarn around cardboard square 15 times. Slide off; tie in middle and clip loops. Glue hair in place along edge of felt. Pull six or eight strands of yarn over face and trim for bangs. Secure hair with dabs of glue. Using dry paintbrush, apply cosmetic blusher to cheeks. Dot on two tiny eyes with black marking pen.

7. Apply glue to end of toothpick; insert head onto toothpick, inserting toothpick at bottom edge of felt face.

8. For wings, tie a bow of six 4" loops from ¼"-wide gold ribbon. Fasten loops with wire; pin to back of neck, trimming ribbon ends.

9. For halo, trim remaining piece of wire-edge ribbon close to wire edge. Wrap wire around edge of quarter and twist ends together; trim to ¼". Make hole in back of head with point of sharpened pencil; apply glue to twisted ends of halo and insert in hole.

10. Tie monofilament into hanging loop; tie loop around pin. Push pin into top of angel's head, concealing pinhead in hair. ●

No-Sew Yo-Yo Banner

You don't have to be a seamstress to turn out spirited holiday decorations like this one! Build a tree from fabric yo-yos and decorate it with buttons and baubles for a one-of-a-kind yuletide banner.

Design by Debbie Rines courtesy of Duncan Enterprises

No-Sew Yo-Yos

1. From brown fabric scrap, cut one 3" circle. From assorted green fabrics, cut nine 3¾", three 3¼" and six 2¾" circles. From red Christmas-print fabric, cut two 2¾" circles.

2. Apply a spot of fabric glue to center of wrong side of a circle. Fold edge facing you to center, touching glue; finger-press straight edge. Fold next edge to the right in same manner. Continue around circle, adding glue whenever needed, until one sharp point is left; fold point to the center. Add more glue to the center and let dry. Repeat for remaining circles.

Banner

1. Arrange green yo-yos on batting in tree shape, using four 3¾" circles for bottom row, three 3¾" circles for next row, three 3¼" circles for next row and a total of six 2¾" circles for next three rows; attach with fabric glue. Glue brown yo-yo at center bottom of tree for trunk.

2. Using jewel glue, glue buttons to centers of yo-yos; glue brass star to top of tree.

3. Cut one 13" x 18" and one 12" x 17" piece of red Christmas-print fabric. Pull threads on all sides of larger piece to make ½" fringe. Following manufacturer's instructions, iron fusible web to wrong side of smaller piece; remove paper backing. Place wrong side of fringed piece over wrong side of smaller piece; fuse.

4. Using fabric glue, glue batting to right side of fringed red Christmas fabric.

5. For hanging loops, cut two 3" x 8½" pieces of green fabric; press raw edges under. Fold in half lengthwise; press. Using fabric glue through step 6, glue edges together. Fold in half again; glue ends to front and back of banner.

6. Glue each 2¾" red yo-yo to center of 3¾" green yo-yo; glue over ends of hanging loops.

7. Using jewel glue, glue buttons to centers of yo-yos; let dry.

8. Place cinnamon stick through hanging loops; tie cording to each end of stick. Fray ends of cording. ❦

Materials

- ½ yard red Christmas-print fabric
- Fabric scraps: brown and assorted greens
- 10" x 14½" piece natural cotton batting
- 11" x 16" Aleene's Fusible Web by Duncan Enterprises
- 1½"-diameter brass star from Creative Beginnings
- 19 assorted colorful buttons
- 13" cinnamon stick
- ⅔ yard twisted satin cording
- Aleene's No-Sew Fabric Glue by Duncan Enterprises
- Aleene's Jewel-It jewel glue by Duncan Enterprises
- Iron

Project Note

Refer to photo throughout for placement.

"Let It Snow" Door Hanger

This cheery project is easy to make with sponges, glitter paint and craft foam!

Design by Creative Chi

Materials

- Wooden door hanger
- 2 (¼"-thick) household sponges
- Americana acrylic paints from DecoArt:
  Snow white #DA1
  Dark pine #DA49
  Kelly green #DA55
  Santa red #DA170
- Starlight crystal #DHH18
  Heavenly Hues paint from DecoArt
- Paintbrush
- 3½" wooden craft pick
- Scraps of craft foam: white, orange, black and red
- Red medium-line permanent marking pen
- ¼" hole punch
- 9" (½"-wide) red/green plaid ribbon
- 3" piece 20-gauge white-wrapped craft wire
- Low-temperature glue gun

Project Note

Refer to photo throughout for placement.

Instructions

1. Base-coat all surfaces of wooden door hanger with dark pine. When dry, sponge with kelly green; let dry. Finish with a coat of crystal paint; let dry.

2. Referring to patterns (page 184), cut pieces from remainder of sponges: one smaller circle for snowman head, one larger circle for body and two crescents for earmuffs. Round off front edges of all sponge pieces by trimming with sharp scissors.

3. Paint snowman head and body with snow white, using two coats if necessary. When paint is dry, finish with a coat of crystal paint; let dry.

4. Using Santa red, paint earmuffs, using two coats if necessary; paint craft pick. Finish earmuffs with a coat of crystal paint.

5. Cut banner from white craft foam; write "Let It Snow" on banner with red marking pen.

6. Using hole punch, punch one circle from orange craft foam, six circles from black and three circles from red.

7. Glue snowman body to head, edge to edge. Tie ribbon around neck; glue snowman to door hanger. Glue wire to door hanger over snowman's head as shown. Position red craft pick for banner pole and glue in place; glue red earmuffs over ends of wire on sides of head.

8. Glue white foam banner in place. Glue on orange foam circle for nose, black foam circles for eyes and mouth, and red circles down front for buttons. ●

Cookies & Milk Set

Santa's face will light up as he sees his Christmas Eve treats served on this charming set!

Designs by Vicki Blizzard

Materials

- Clear glass footed mug
- Clear glass dinner plate
- Expandable sponge
- Perm Enamel glass surface conditioner from Delta Technical Coatings Inc.
- Air-Dry Perm Enamel paints from Delta Technical Coatings Inc.:
  Burnt sienna #45-010-0202
  Cotton candy pink #45-015-0202
  Hunter green #45-032-0202
  Ultra white #45-029-0202
  Red red #45-033-0202
  Ultra black #45-034-0202
- 3/0 liner brush
- Pencil
- Paper plate

Project Notes

Let paints dry before applying adjacent or overlaying colors.

All paint is applied to outside of mug and to wrong side of plate.

Mug

1. Apply surface conditioner to outside of mug, following manufacturer's instructions.

2. Referring to patterns (page 185), cut one small heart and one small gingerbread man from expandable sponge. Expand sponges in water; squeeze until almost dry.

3. Use paper plate for palette. Pour a small puddle of burnt sienna onto paper plate. Press gingerbread man sponge into paint and stamp a line of gingerbread men around outside of mug so their hands almost touch.

4. Pour red red paint onto plate; using heart sponge, stamp a heart over each pair of hands.

5. Using liner brush throughout, paint round, cotton candy pink cheeks on each gingerbread man.

6. Using red red, paint wavy line around top of mug; dot on buttons and paint a smile on each gingerbread man.

7. Using hunter green, paint bow tie on each gingerbread man; add dots in each curve of red wavy line.

8. Using ultra white, add hair and leg trim to each gingerbread man; add dots to hearts.

Plate

1. Apply surface conditioner to wrong side of plate, following manufacturer's instructions.

2. Referring to template, cut one large gingerbread man from expandable sponge. Expand sponge in water; squeeze until almost dry.

3. Lay sponge on work surface. Turn plate over and place right side down over sponge, centering sponge under plate. Using liner brush and red red paint, paint gingerbread man's smile, three buttons and small red heart on one leg. Paint cotton candy pink cheeks, hunter green bow tie, ultra black eyes and ultra white hair and trim on arms and legs.

4. Pour thin layer of burnt sienna paint onto paper plate. Dip large gingerbread sponge into paint and place sponge paint side up on work surface. Turn plate over so right side is facing up and press wrong side (painted surface) of plate onto painted sponge, carefully centering painted details within gingerbread man. Lift off plate; place right side down to dry. If desired, add a second coat of burnt sienna to fill in open areas on gingerbread man.

5. Using liner brush throughout, outline gingerbread man with ultra black.

6. Paint red red wavy outline around plate rim; add forest green dots in each curve of wave.

7. Cut 2" square of expandable sponge; expand in water and squeeze out excess water. Pour a thin layer of ultra white paint onto paper plate; press sponge into paint and sponge over back of plate, repeating until plate is covered with as much paint as is desired. ❦

Festive Felt Cookies

Fun, fanciful and definitely low-cal, these colorful felt "cookies" will look delectable on your tree, or scrumptious decorating your gifts! Young crafters will have a ball with these.

Designs by Leslie Hartsock

Materials

- 9" x 12" sheets Rainbow felt from Kunin Felt:
  Antique white #379
  White #550
  Walnut brown #8H3
  Cashmere tan #884
  Ruby #0H1
  Baby pink #053
  Copper #065
- PeelnStick double-sided adhesive by Therm O Web
- Iridescent multicolored glitter
- Fine glitter: red and green
- 15mm round faceted cabochons from The Beadery: 1 each ruby red and emerald green
- Shiny white Scribbles dimensional fabric paint by Duncan Enterprises
- 6-strand embroidery floss: red, green and white
- 6 (6"-long) pieces assorted ribbon or floss (for hangers)
- Pinking shears or decorative-edge scissors
- Large-eye embroidery needle
- Clear-drying craft glue
- All-purpose paintbrush

Project Note

Refer to photo throughout.

Gingerbread Star

1. Cut two 4" squares copper felt. Following manufacturer's instructions, adhere to one another with 4" square double-sided adhesive. Referring to patterns (page 186), trace gingerbread star pattern onto felt; cut out on traced line using pinking shears or decorative-edge scissors.

2. Dot shiny white dimensional fabric paint randomly over front of star; let dry.

3. Paint a film of clear-drying craft glue over front of star; sprinkle with iridescent multicolored glitter.

4. Fold 6" piece ribbon or floss in half for hanger; glue ends to back of star. Let dry.

Pink Sugar Wafer

1. Fold 6" piece ribbon or floss in half. Cut two 3½" x 1" pieces from baby pink felt; following manufacturer's instructions, adhere to one another with 3½" x 1" piece double-sided adhesive, sandwiching ends of folded ribbon between layers at one end.

2. Run a thin line of clear-drying craft glue in crisscross design over top of cookie; sprinkle with iridescent multicolored glitter, shaking off excess. Let dry.

Pinwheel Cookies

1. Using pinking shears or decorative-edge scissors, cut two 3½" squares from antique white felt. Mark center of each square with pencil dot; cut from each corner to approximately ¼" from center dot.

2. Glue every other corner tip at center of square. Apply clear-drying craft glue to unfolded tips; sprinkle one cookie with green glitter and the other with red, shaking off excess. Let dry.

3. Glue red faceted cabochon to center of green-glittered cookie, and green faceted cabochon to center of red-glittered cookie. Let dry.

4. Thread embroidery needle with 6" piece of ribbon or floss; pull through tip of cookie. Knot ends for hanger. Repeat for remaining cookie shape.

Sprinkle Cookie

1. Referring to patterns (page 186), cut two large circles from cashmere tan felt and one from double-sided adhesive. Using 6 strands red, green and white floss, randomly embroider straight stitches to resemble cookie sprinkles on front of one circle.

2. Fold 6" piece ribbon in half for hanger. Following manufacturer's instructions, adhere unstitched circle to

wrong side of embroidered circle with double-sided adhesive, sandwiching ends of hanging ribbon between felt layers.

3. Paint a thin film of clear-drying craft glue over front of cookie; sprinkle with iridescent multicolored glitter, shaking off excess. Let dry.

Spiral Cookie

1. Fold 6" piece ribbon in half for hanger. Referring to patterns (page 186), cut two large circles from walnut brown felt and one from double-sided adhesive. Following manufacturer's instructions, adhere felt circles to one another with double-sided adhesive, sandwiching ends of hanging ribbon between layers.

2. Cut a 3" square of white felt and another from double-sided adhesive. Following manufacturer's instructions, apply one side of adhesive to wrong side of felt square. Cut spiral from adhesive-backed felt; remove paper backing from adhesive. Beginning at center, adhere white spiral to cookie shape, separating edges slightly to allow brown to show through.

3. Paint a thin film of clear-drying craft glue on front of cookie; sprinkle with iridescent multicolored glitter, shaking off excess. Let dry.

Rolling Pin Cookie

1. Cut one 2½" x 3" piece each from cashmere tan felt and double-sided adhesive. Cut one 2½" x 4" piece each from ruby felt and double-sided adhesive.

2. Following manufacturer's instructions, apply adhesive to wrong side of each felt piece. Remove paper backing from adhesive on ruby felt; beginning at long edge, roll up felt into a tight cylinder.

3. Remove paper backing from cashmere felt; center ruby roll over one long edge of cashmere tan felt. Roll cashmere tan felt around ruby felt.

4. Thread embroidery needle with 6" piece of ribbon; pull through tip of cookie. Knot ends for hanger.

5. Apply thin coat of clear-drying craft glue over cashmere tan felt; sprinkle with iridescent multicolored glitter, shaking off excess. Let dry. 🔔

Scrap-Quilt Ornaments

Transform a plain, old, brown paper bag and a few fabric scraps into positively charming holiday trims with a cozy country feel.

Designs by Helen L. Rafson

Materials

- Fabric scraps: pink and gold solid, red, green, gold, blue and brown prints, and gold lamé
- Brown paper bag
- Fusible transfer web
- Jute twine
- Ultra-fine-line black marking pen
- Polyester fiberfill or other stuffing
- Craft glue
- Iron

Project Note

Refer to photo throughout for placement.

Instructions

1. Following manufacturer's instructions, fuse transfer webbing onto wrong sides of fabrics.

2. Referring to patterns (page 149), cut two background pieces for each design—tree, angel, house and star—from heavy brown paper. (Reverse one angel pattern if needed to avoid having printing from bag on right side of ornament.)

3. Referring to patterns, cut appliqués from fused fabrics:

Angel—Cut gown sections and sleeve from red print, wings from gold lamé, hair from gold print, trumpet from gold solid, and face and hand from pink solid.

Star—Cut one section from each of five different fabrics.

House—Cut house front from blue print, roof from green print, side from red print and windows and door from gold print.

Tree—Cut tree sections from green print and trunk from brown print.

4. Remove paper backing from appliqués; fuse to brown paper backgrounds.

5. Using marking pen, draw dashed lines around each fabric appliqué to resemble running stitch.

6. Glue small amount of fiberfill to back of each appliquéd piece; let dry. For each ornament, fold 8" length of jute twine in half; glue ends to back of appliquéd piece; let dry.

7. Glue brown paper fronts and backs together around edges. Let dry. ●

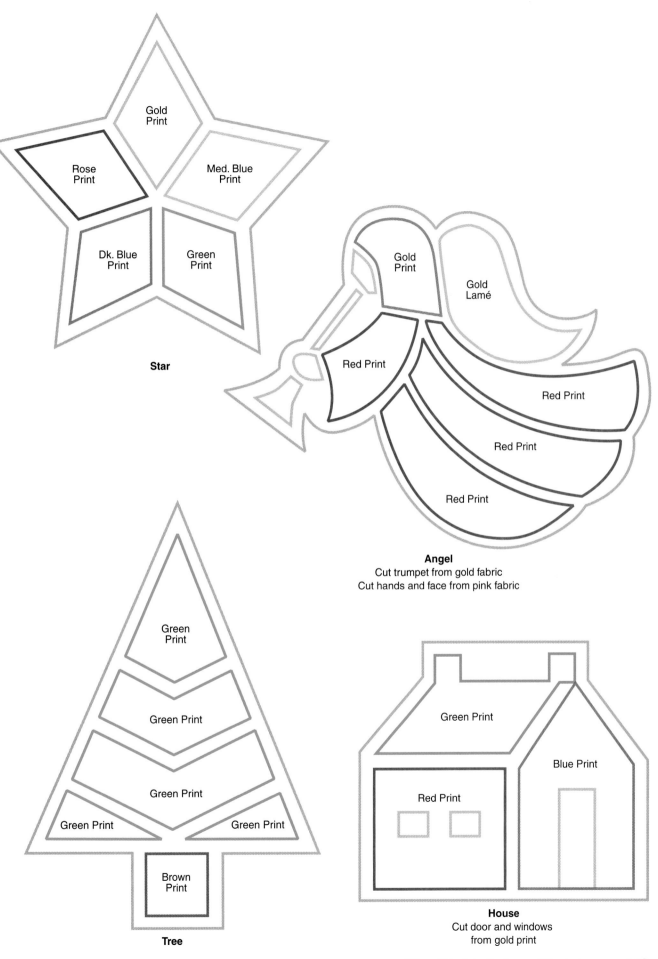

Star

Angel
Cut trumpet from gold fabric
Cut hands and face from pink fabric

Gold Print

Gold Lamé

Red Print

Red Print

Red Print

Red Print

Gold Print

Rose Print

Med. Blue Print

Dk. Blue Print

Green Print

Green Print

Green Print

Green Print

Green Print

Green Print

Brown Print

Tree

Green Print

Blue Print

Red Print

House
Cut door and windows
from gold print

Pattern Index

Special Thanks

Much thanks to the wonderfully talented designers who contributed their original craft designs to this book. It has been an honor and pleasure to feature their work. —Laura Scott, editor

Judy Atwell
Mary Ayres
Judith Barker
Martha Bleidner of Creative Chi
Vicki Blizzard
Janna Britton
Deborah Brooks
Mary Cosgrove
Carol Dace
Louy Danube
Sandy Dye
Joan Fee

Leslie Hartsock
Jackie Haskell
Heather Bell Henry
Doxie Keller
Annie Lang
Celia Lange of Creative Chi
Margi Laurin
Chris Malone
Nancy Marshall
Janice McKee
Rochelle Norris
Helen Rafson

Debbie Rines
Joanna Randolph Rott
Delores Ruzicka
Sandra Graham Smith
Bonnie Stephens
Florence Bolen Tebbets
Sharon Tittle
Donna Vailes
Kathy Wegner
Beth Wheeler
Angie Wilhite
Barbara Woolley

Country Angel Ornaments
Continued from page 10

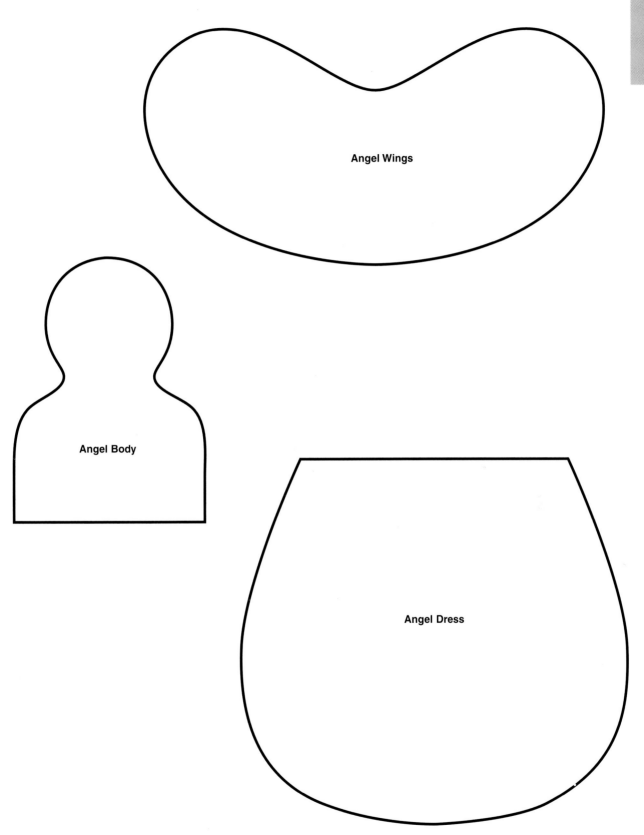

Angel Wings

Angel Body

Angel Dress

Bee and Hive Plant Pokes

Continued from page 13

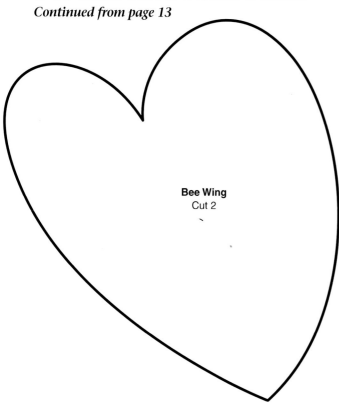

Bee Wing
Cut 2

egg. Apply glue to black egg and insert onto toothpicks for bee's head.

5. Using black dimensional paint, scatter clusters of three dots over yellow portion of body.

6. Using a craft stick, carefully gouge a comma shape into each side of body to receive wings; apply glue to

wings and insert into body, using craft stick to help position wings in the grooves.

7. Apply a little glue to ends of antennae and insert into head. Add oval eyes with yellow dimensional paint; let dry and dot on pupils with black dimensional paint.

8. Apply glue to one end of dowel; insert in underside of bee's body.

9. Tie several strands of raffia in a bow around dowel; glue to underside of bee to hold in place.

Hive

1. Flatten wide end of egg on a smooth, flat surface. Apply dot of glue to center of flattened bottom; begin wrapping egg with jute at this point. Keep applying glue to egg and coiling jute, winding the strands evenly to cover egg. Continue wrapping until only about ¼" of plastic foam shows at top of egg.

2. Leave a 3" tail of jute and cut off remaining excess. Using tips of blunt scissors or a pencil, stuff end of twine into top of egg, leaving a loop. Apply glue to top of egg to hold twine in place.

3. Paint 1½" x 1¾" oval on one side of hive using black paint; let dry.

4. Glue ivy leaves to one side of painted oval and to top of egg.

5. Curl wire stems of violets around pencil; slide off and glue violets around ivy, leaving curled tendrils protruding. Glue resin bee on other side of painted oval.

6. To finish hive, repeat steps 8 and 9 for bee. ❋

Friendly Felt Beanbag Pets

Continued from page 22

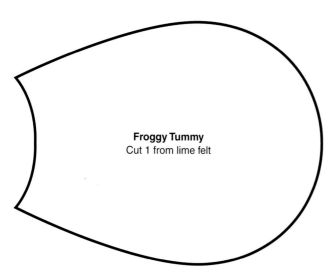

Froggy Tummy
Cut 1 from lime felt

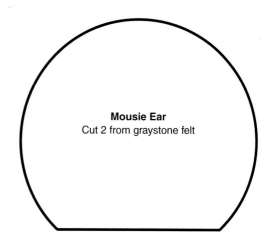

Mousie Ear
Cut 2 from graystone felt

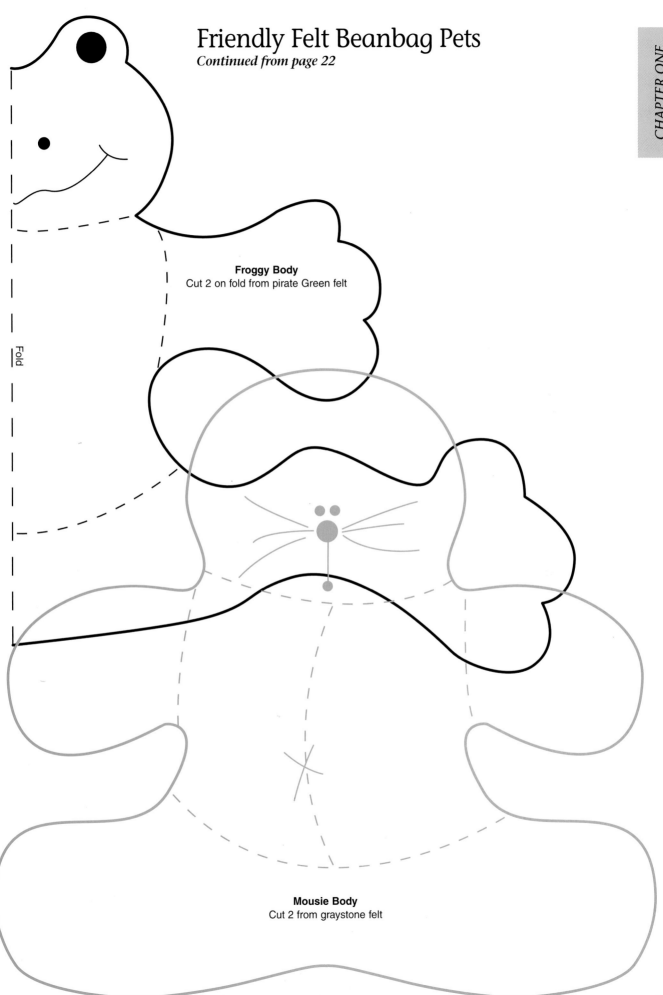

Friendly Felt Beanbag Pets

Continued from page 22

Fold

Froggy Body
Cut 2 on fold from pirate Green felt

Mousie Body
Cut 2 from graystone felt

Scrub-a-Dub-Dub!

Continued from page 24

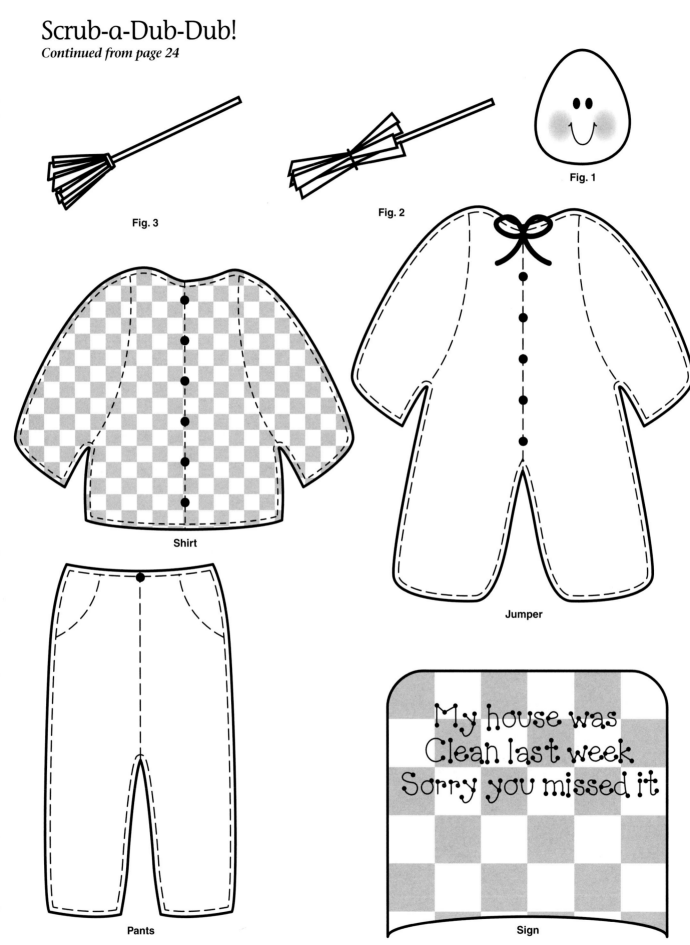

Fig. 3

Fig. 2

Fig. 1

Shirt

Jumper

Pants

Sign

My house was
Clean last week
Sorry you missed it

Valentine Heart Box

Continued from page 29

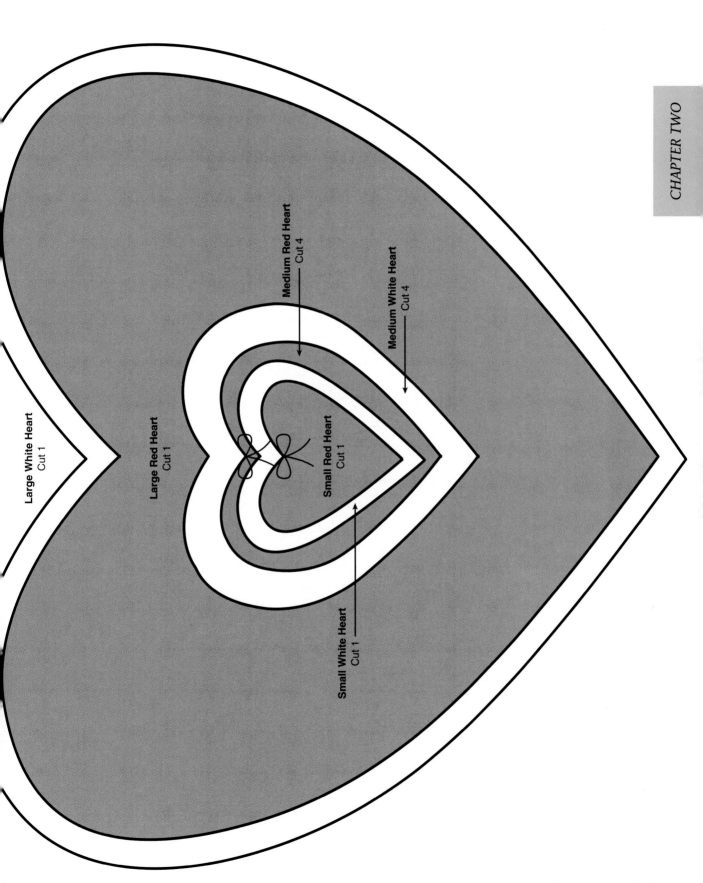

Large White Heart
Cut 1

Large Red Heart
Cut 1

Medium Red Heart
Cut 4

Medium White Heart
Cut 4

Small Red Heart
Cut 1

Small White Heart
Cut 1

Enlarge Drawing 155%
to return to original size

Special Mum

Continued from page 37

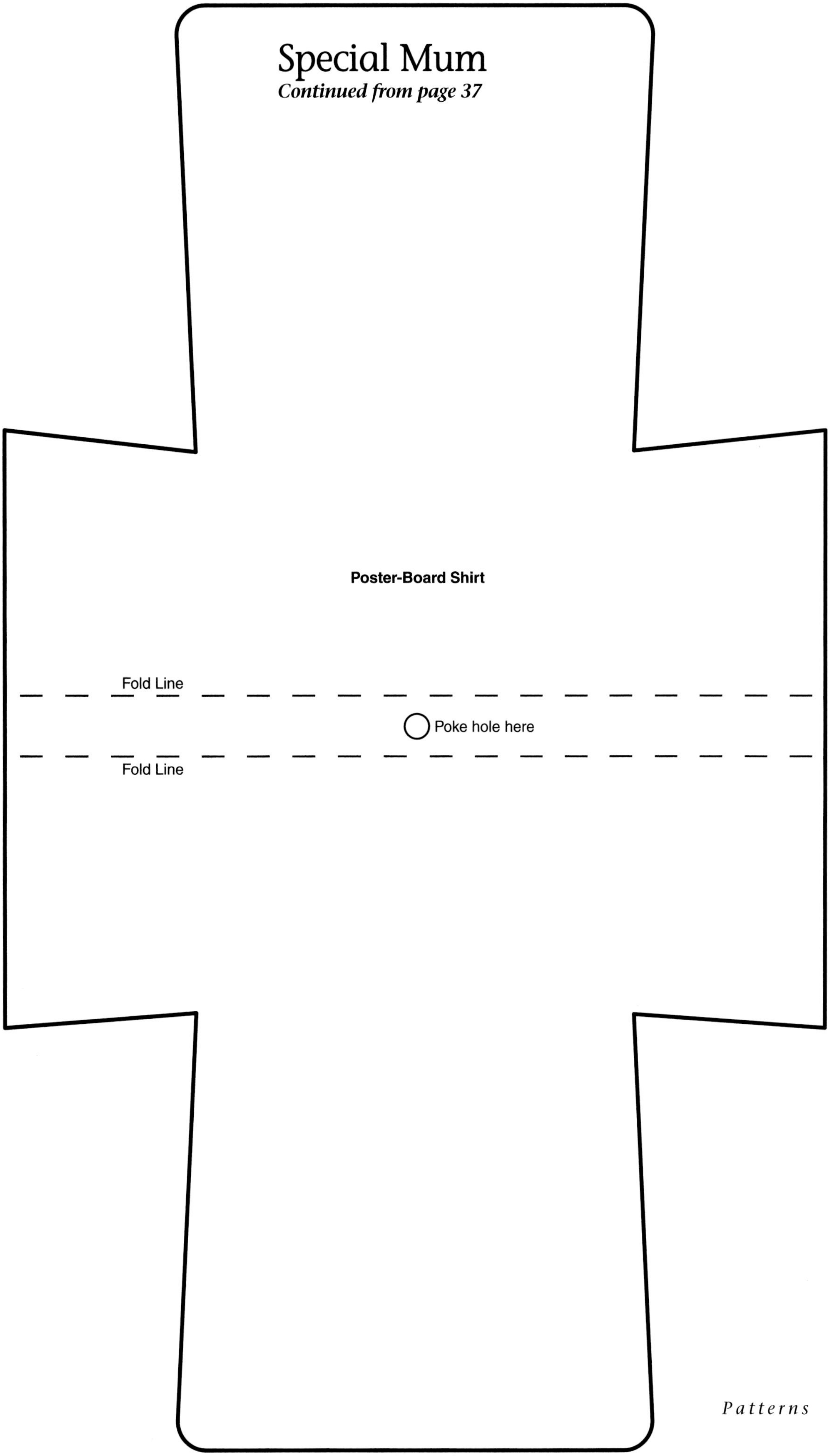

Poster-Board Shirt

Fold Line -

◯ Poke hole here

Fold Line -

Special Mum

Continued from page 37

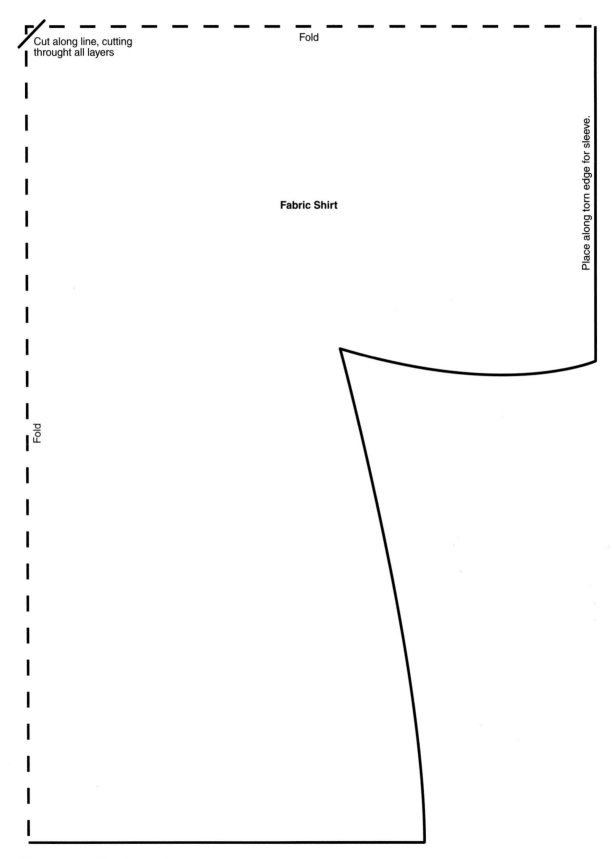

Cut along line, cutting throught all layers

Fold

Fabric Shirt

Place along torn edge for sleeve.

Fold

Teddy Bear Pocket Purse

Continued from page 44

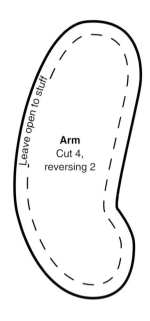

Arm
Cut 4,
reversing 2

Leave open to stuff

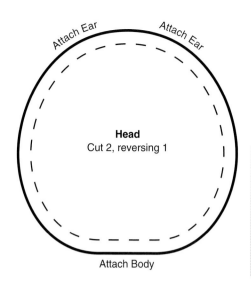

Attach Ear   Attach Ear

Head
Cut 2, reversing 1

Attach Body

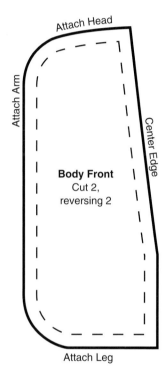

Attach Head

Attach Arm

Body Front
Cut 2,
reversing 2

Center Edge

Attach Leg

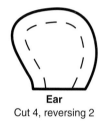

Ear
Cut 4, reversing 2

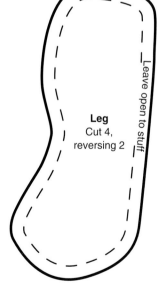

Leg
Cut 4,
reversing 2

Leave open to stuff

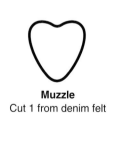

Muzzle
Cut 1 from denim felt

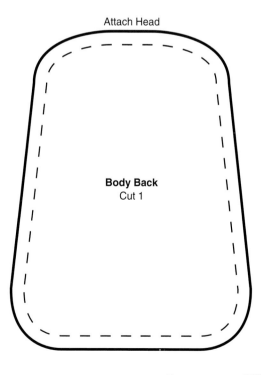

Attach Head

Body Back
Cut 1

Summer Fun Baby Bibs
Continued from page 49

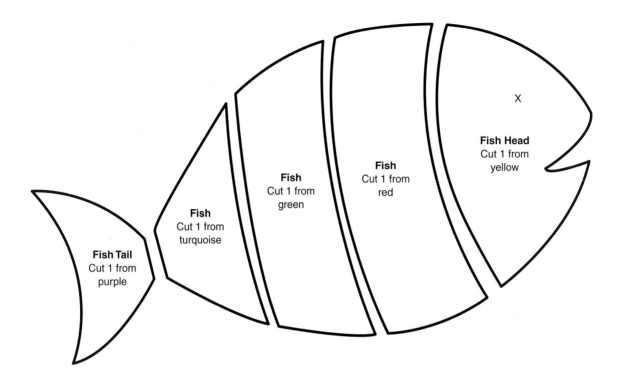

Fish Head
Cut 1 from
yellow

X

Fish
Cut 1 from
red

Fish
Cut 1 from
green

Fish
Cut 1 from
turquoise

Fish Tail
Cut 1 from
purple

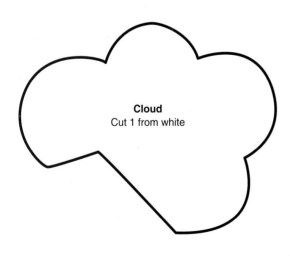

Cloud
Cut 1 from white

Catch of the Day Frame
Continued from page 53

3. Glue chopstick in place. Glue button in place for reel, gluing one end of fishing line under it. Arrange fishing line along right side and across top of frame as desired; hold in place by spot-gluing, applying tiny amounts of glue with the tip of a toothpick.

4. Using wire cutters, remove hooks from fishing flies. Position one fly at the end of the fishing line and the other on the fishing line close to the upper right corner; glue in place.

Kitty Cat Vest
Continued from page 57

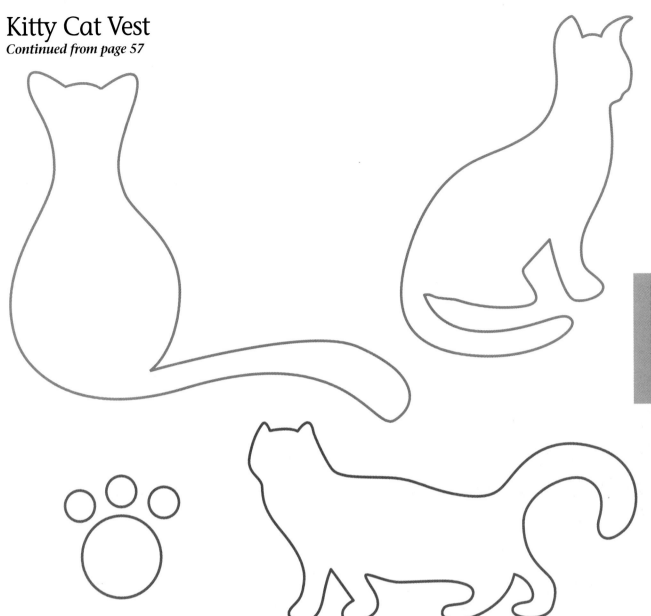

Stars & Cats T-Shirt
Continued from page 57

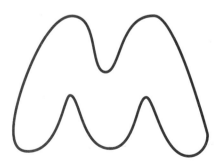
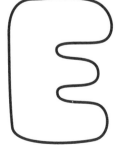
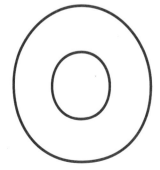

Stars & Cats T-Shirt

Continued from page 57

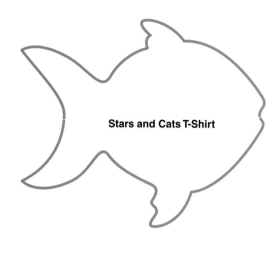

Stars and Cats T-Shirt

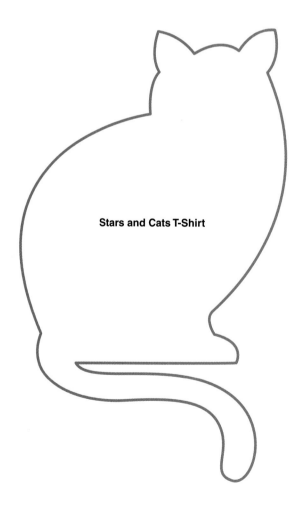

Stars and Cats T-Shirt

All-Star Dad Sweatshirt

Continued from page 63

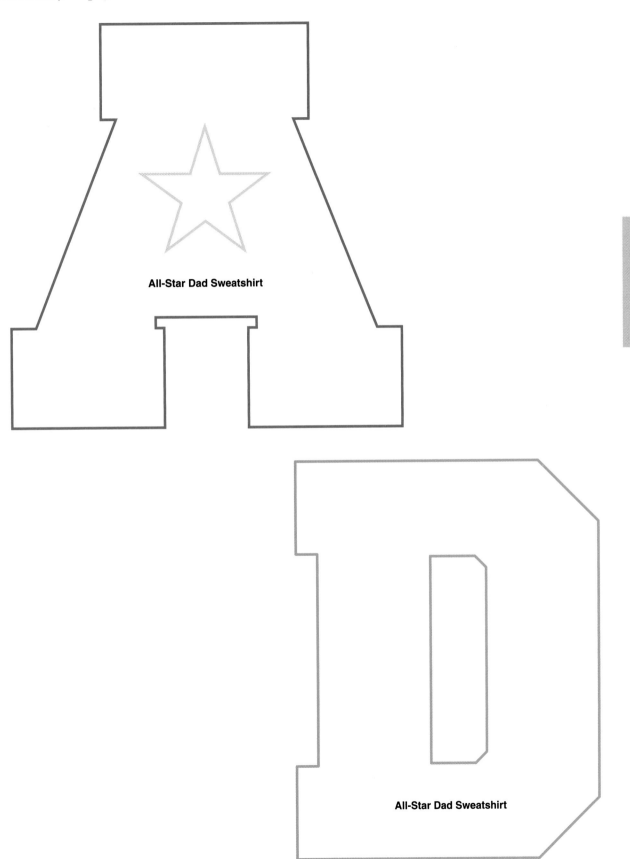

All-Star Dad Sweatshirt

All-Star Dad Sweatshirt

Gum Ball Vest
Continued from page 66

Gum-Ball Machine

Moo-Cows Shorts Set
Continued from page 67

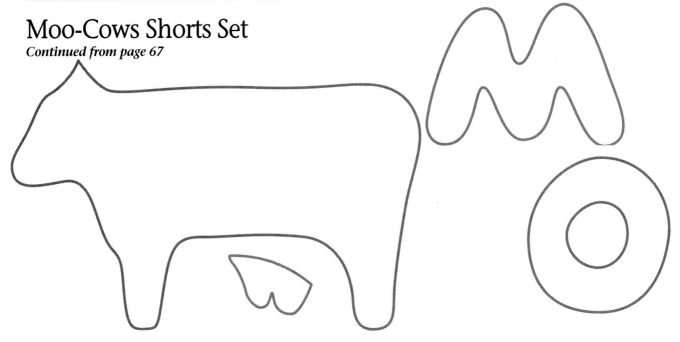

Farmer Bunny & His Bride

Continued from page 71

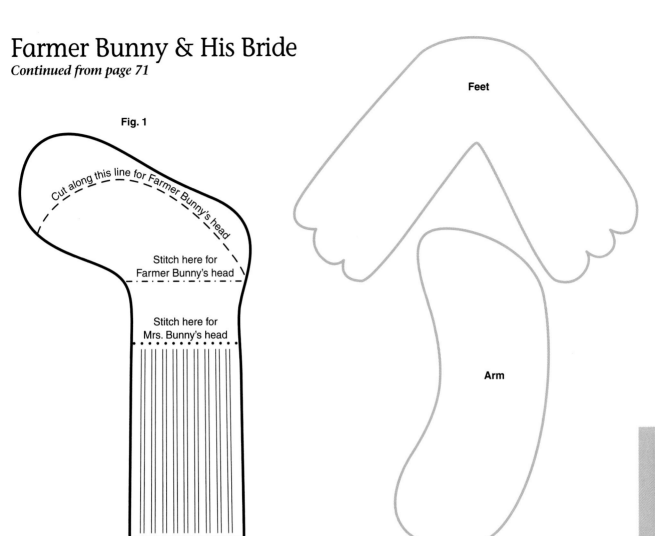

Fig. 1

Cut along this line for Farmer Bunny's head

Stitch here for
Farmer Bunny's head

Stitch here for
Mrs. Bunny's head

Feet

Arm

Beaded Memory Album

Continued from page 73

to fit inside covers, measuring 1½" in from top and bottom edges, ¾" in from outer edge, and long enough to be tucked under edge of metal spine (felt may tuck under more easily if you cut that edge with a regular scissors). Secure top, bottom and side edges of felt with fabric glue. Use screwdriver to ease inner edge under metal spine, over trim (ends of trim should be concealed under felt). Secure this edge of felt with glue as needed. ▪

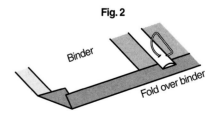

Fig. 1

Binder

Tape

Fold

Fold edge over ¼" and fold over binder

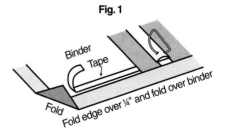

Fig. 2

Binder

Fold over binder

"Gone Fishing" Pillow

Continued from page 75

Back Fin
Cut 1 for each fish
from Fabric B

Side Fin
Cut 1 for each fish
from Fabric B

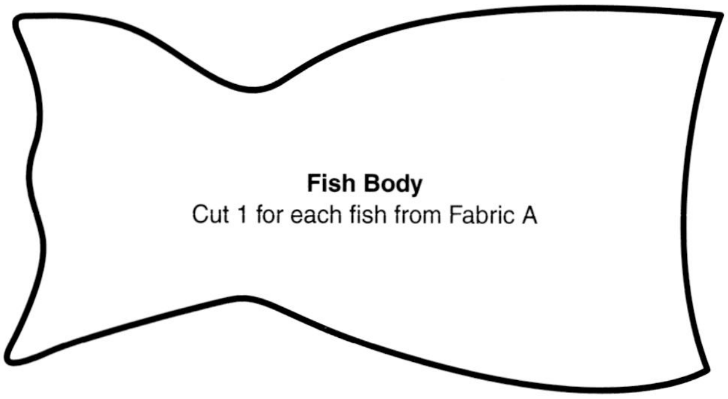

Fish Body
Cut 1 for each fish from Fabric A

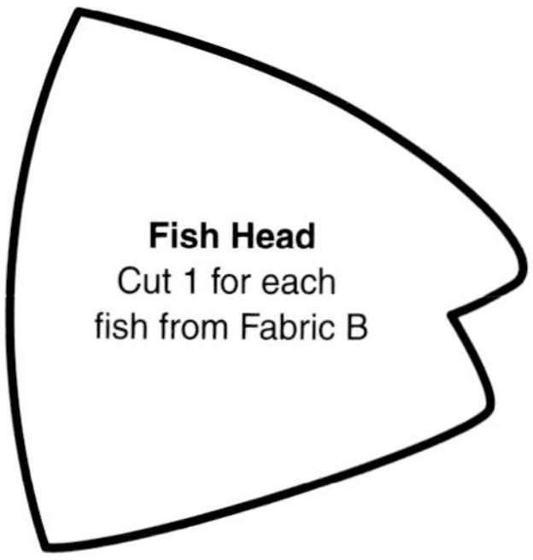

Fish Head
Cut 1 for each
fish from Fabric B

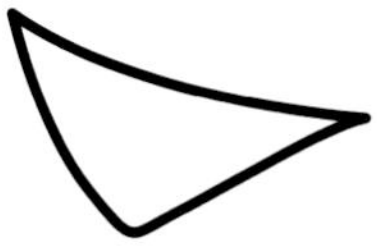

Bottom Fin
Cut 1 for each fish
from Fabric B

N

I

G O S

G

H E F

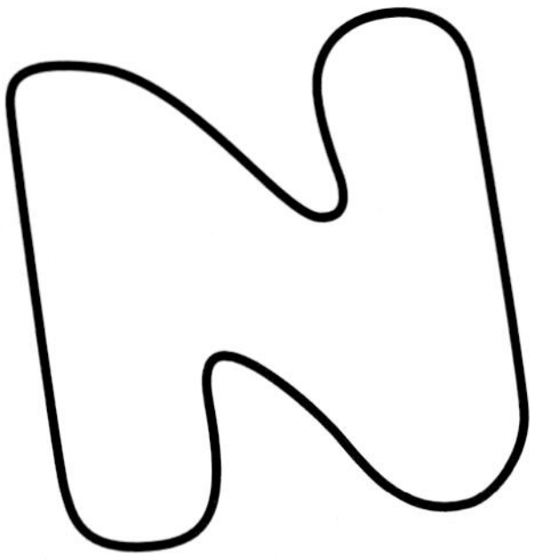

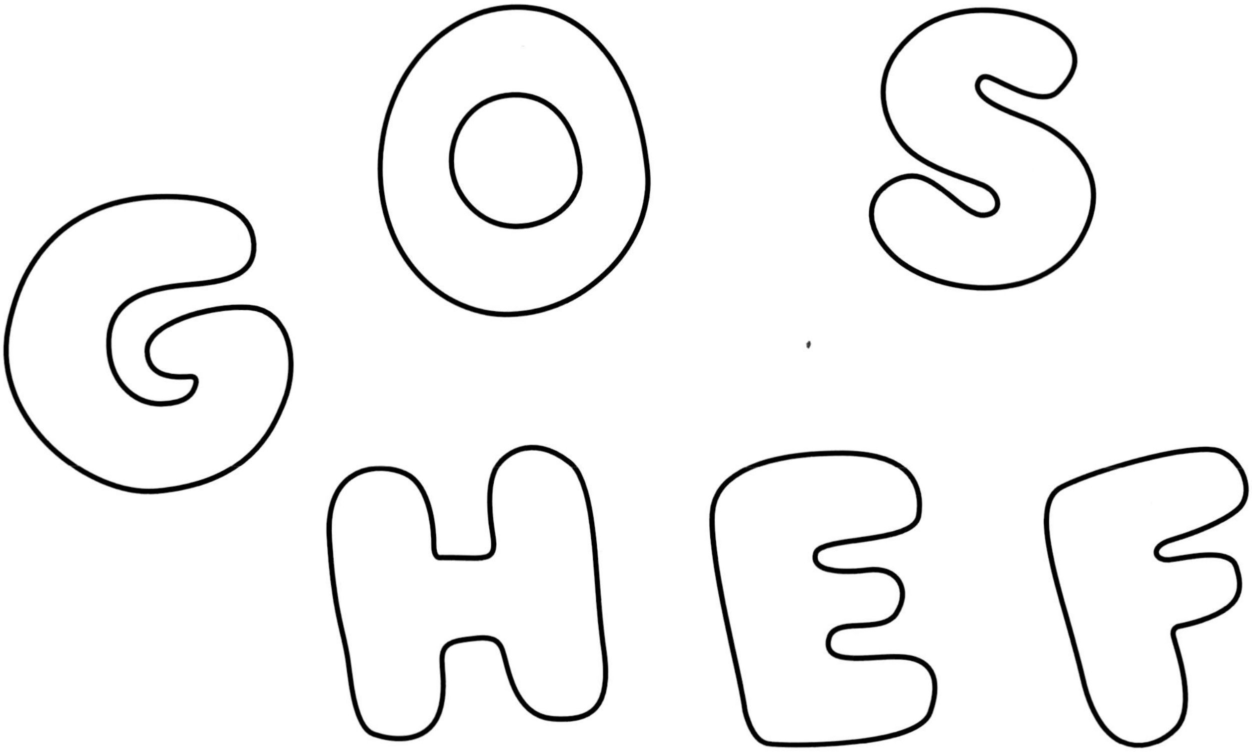

Chenille Chickens

Continued from page 76

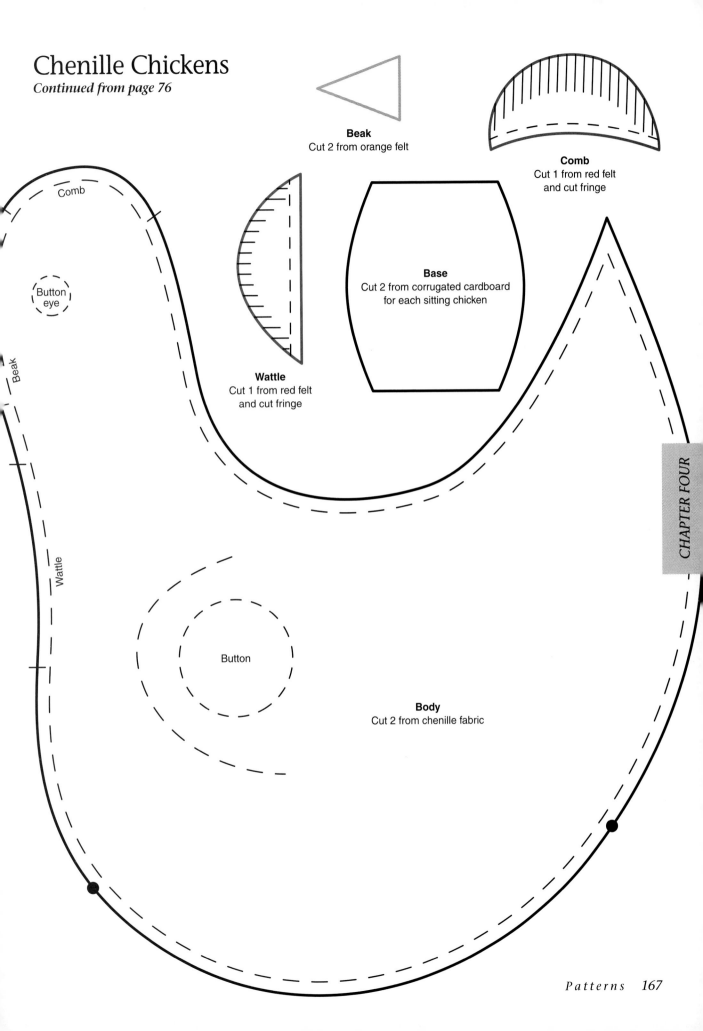

Beak
Cut 2 from orange felt

Comb
Cut 1 from red felt
and cut fringe

Comb

Button
eye

Beak

Wattle

Wattle
Cut 1 from red felt
and cut fringe

Base
Cut 2 from corrugated cardboard
for each sitting chicken

Button

Body
Cut 2 from chenille fabric

Chenille Chickens
Continued from page 77

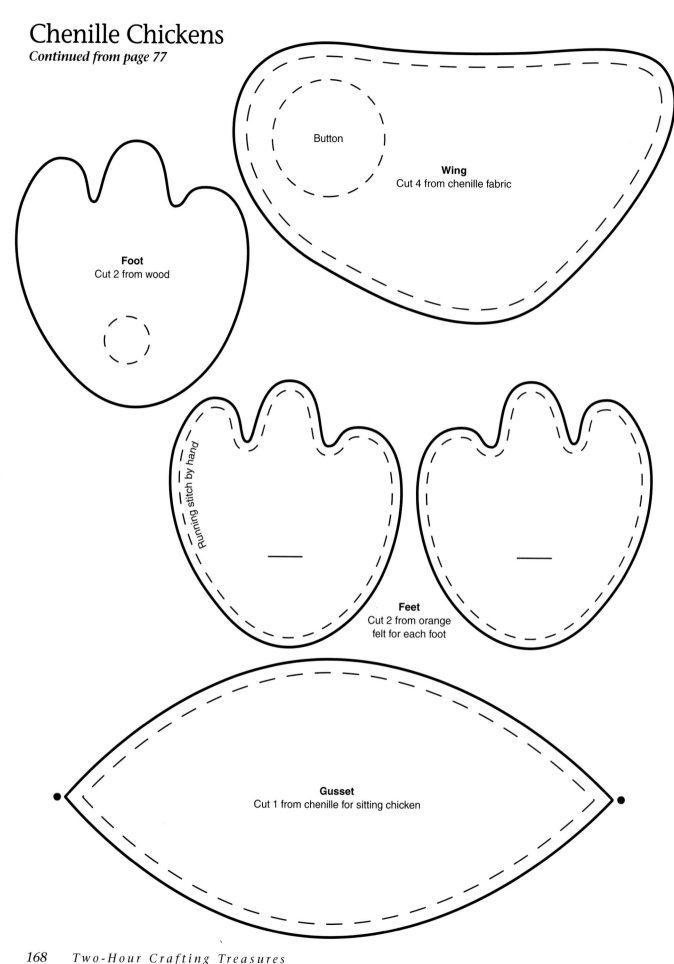

Foot
Cut 2 from wood

Button

Wing
Cut 4 from chenille fabric

Running stitch by hand

Feet
Cut 2 from orange
felt for each foot

Gusset
Cut 1 from chenille for sitting chicken

Patriotic Plant Pokes
Continued from page 79

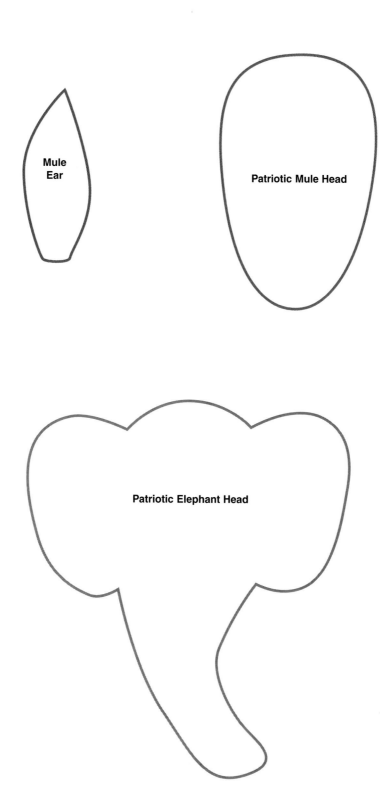

Mule
Ear

Patriotic Mule Head

Patriotic Elephant Head

Nuts About Animals!

Continued from page 86

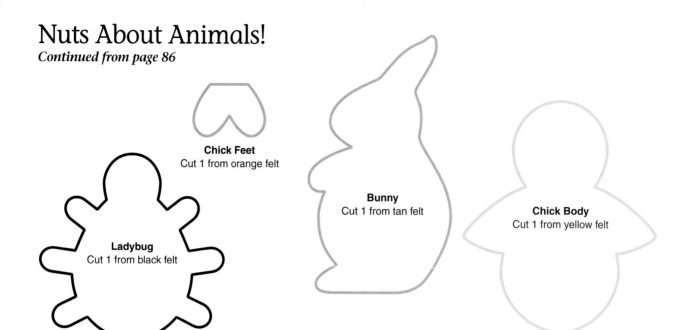

Chick Feet
Cut 1 from orange felt

Bunny
Cut 1 from tan felt

Chick Body
Cut 1 from yellow felt

Ladybug
Cut 1 from black felt

All-Star Photo Frame

Continued from page 87

Golf Ball

Tennis Ball

Baseball

Basketball

Soccer Ball

Noah's Ark Stand-ups

Continued from page 90

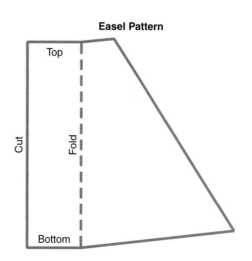

Easel Pattern

Top

Cut

Fold

Bottom

Cute as a Bug Puppets
Continued from page 91

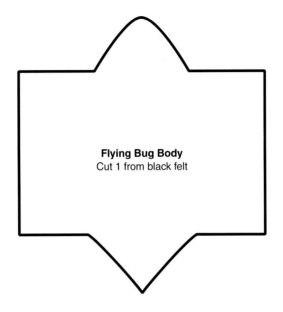

Flying Bug Body
Cut 1 from black felt

Flying Bug Wings
Cut 1 from yellow felt and 1 from orange felt

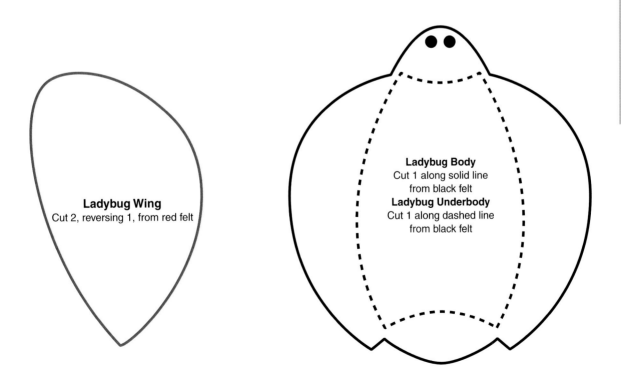

Ladybug Wing
Cut 2, reversing 1, from red felt

Ladybug Body
Cut 1 along solid line
from black felt
Ladybug Underbody
Cut 1 along dashed line
from black felt

CHAPTER FIVE

Candelit Seasons
Continued from page 98

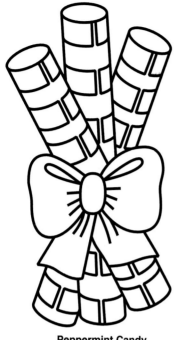

Peppermint Candy

Spring Egg

Autumn Leaf

Summer Flower

St. Pat's Pin & Napkin Ring
Continued from page 104

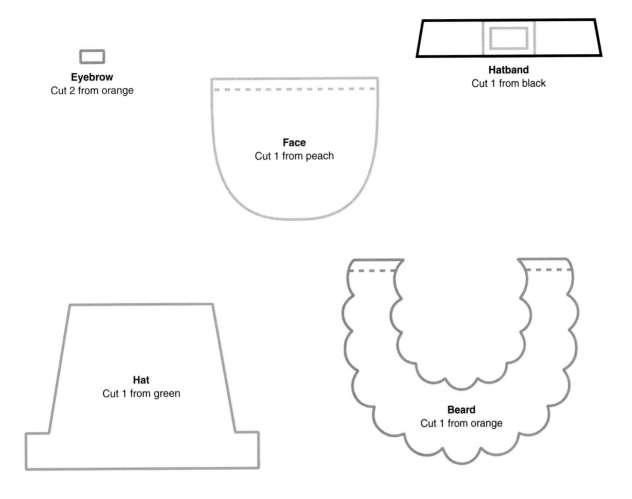

Eyebrow
Cut 2 from orange

Face
Cut 1 from peach

Hatband
Cut 1 from black

Hat
Cut 1 from green

Beard
Cut 1 from orange

Easter Chick Treat Jar
Continued from page 109

Face
Cut 1 from yellow craft foam

Wing
Cut 2 from yellow craft foam

Easter Basket Greeting Card
Continued from page 110

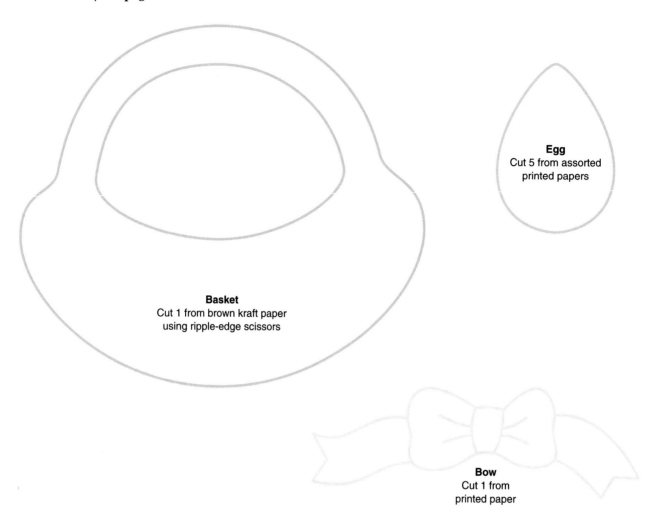

Egg
Cut 5 from assorted
printed papers

Basket
Cut 1 from brown kraft paper
using ripple-edge scissors

Bow
Cut 1 from
printed paper

Blooming Beauties Frame
Continued from page 111

Small Rose
Make 4

Large Rose
Make 2

Pierced Paper Creation
Continued from page 113

Bookmark

Greeting Card

Father's Day Pencil Holder
Continued from page 115

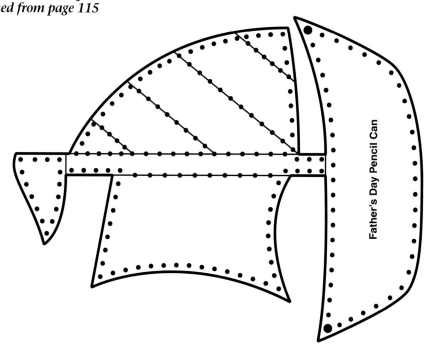

Father's Day Pencil Can

Nine Men's Morris Game

Continued from page 117

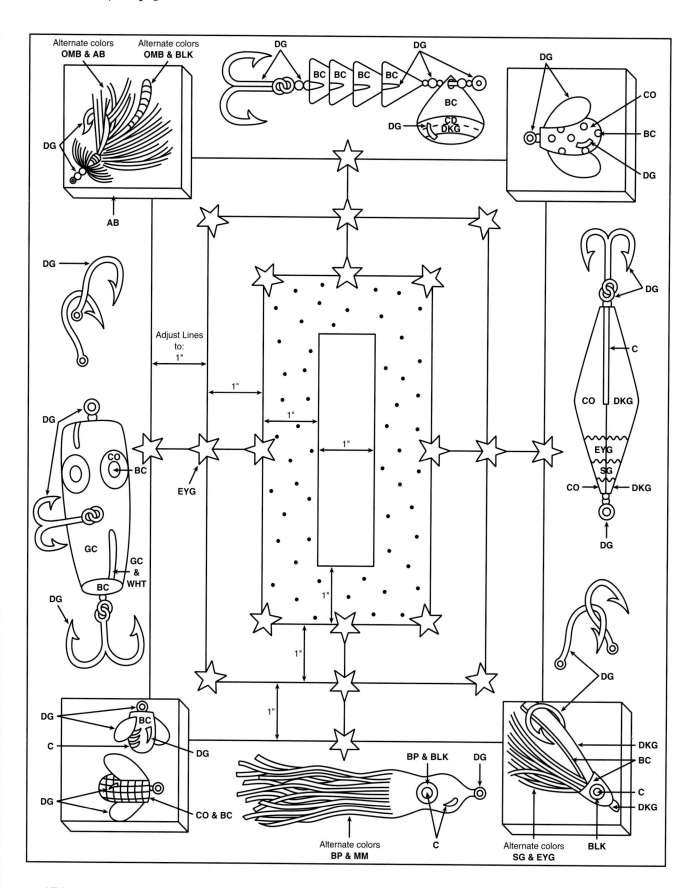

Playing Instructions
Nine Men's Morris

Nine Men's Morris is now going on its 3,000th year of popularity—give or take. The first board ever discovered was carved by workmen into a temple under construction in ancient Egypt. Later on, the game found its way into the Talmud, King Alfonso's 13th century *Book of Games* and Shakespeare's *A Midsummer Night's Dream.* Over the years, and throughout the world, Nine Men's Morris has been a "fad" countless times. If ever there were an all-time classic game, this would have to be it.

COLOR KEY	
WHT	White
DG	Drizzle grey
C	Custard
SP	Silver pine
CO	Calypso orange
BC	Black cherry
DKG	Dark goldenrod
EYG	English yew green
MM	Misty mauve
AB	Autumn brown
GC	Georgia clay
BLK	Black
BP	Bouquet pink
OMB	Ocean mist blue
SG	Spring green

2 Players

To Start: Players start with 9 pieces each, and the board starts empty.

Setting Up: Taking turns, players put all their pieces, one at a time, on 18 vacant points (stars) on the board.

Having accomplished that, players continue taking turns. A turn consists of moving a piece along a line to an adjacent empty point.

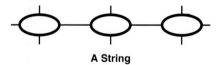

A String

Making a String: A string is a complete line-up of 3 pieces—same color—filling all 3 points of a line. Any line counts. Players can make a string either during set-up phase or during play.

Once a player has managed to build a string, he or she is immediately allowed to grab any enemy piece. The only limitation: an enemy piece from an enemy string may not be removed—unless no other piece is available.

It's legal to break up one of your own strings by moving one of its pieces out and then—if your opponent is napping and doesn't block—putting it back in place on a later move, thereby re-forming the same string all over. If you succeed, you can claim another enemy piece.

Winning: A player wins by getting his or her opponent down to 2 pieces. A player also wins if an opponent is blocked so that no move can be made.

Optional Rule: A player who has only 3 pieces remaining is allowed, on turn, to move any one of his pieces to any vacant space. This is known as "flying" and it's designed to give the underdog a fighting chance.

Rockets' Red Glare Apron
Continued from page 118

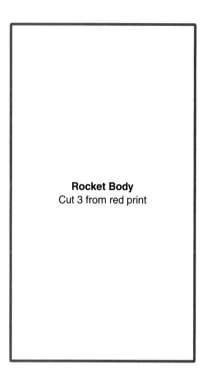

Rocket Body
Cut 3 from red print

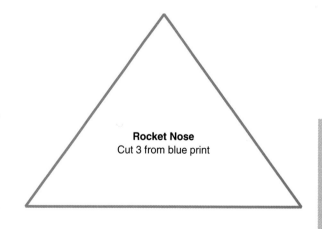

Rocket Nose
Cut 3 from blue print

Patriotic Memo Holder

Continued from page 120

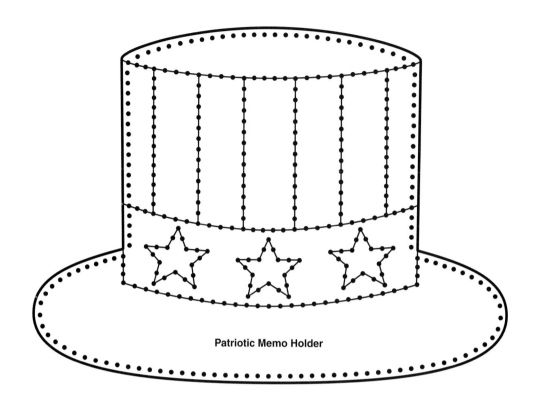

Patriotic Memo Holder

Sammy Scarecrow Hanging

Continued from page 122

Boo!
Enlarge 167%

Sammy Scarecrow
Enlarge 167%

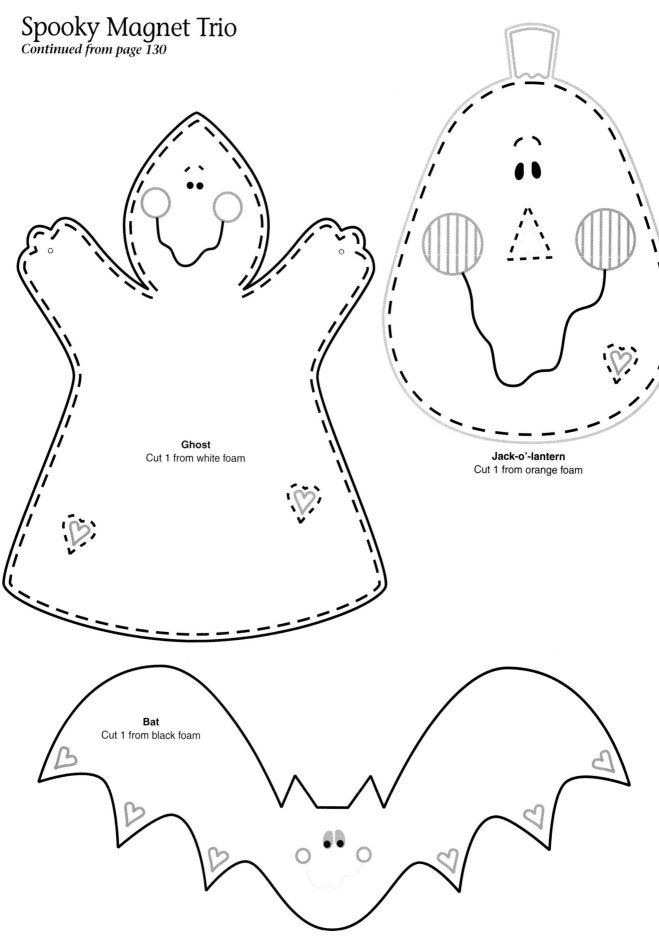

Ghost
Cut 1 from white foam

Jack-o'-lantern
Cut 1 from orange foam

Bat
Cut 1 from black foam

Fall Spendor Place Settings

Continued from page 132

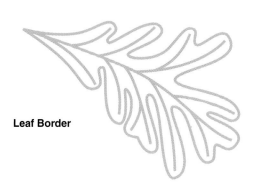

Leaf Border

Leaf Cluster

Felt Snowman & Santa
Continued from page 135

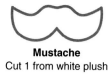

Mustache
Cut 1 from white plush

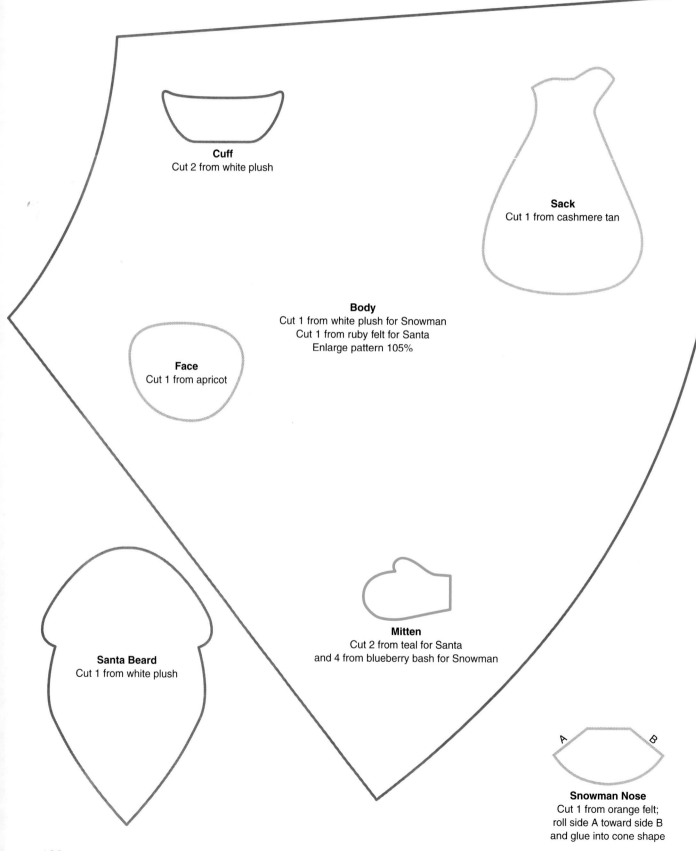

Cuff
Cut 2 from white plush

Sack
Cut 1 from cashmere tan

Body
Cut 1 from white plush for Snowman
Cut 1 from ruby felt for Santa
Enlarge pattern 105%

Face
Cut 1 from apricot

Santa Beard
Cut 1 from white plush

Mitten
Cut 2 from teal for Santa
and 4 from blueberry bash for Snowman

A   B

Snowman Nose
Cut 1 from orange felt;
roll side A toward side B
and glue into cone shape

Festive Gift Bags
Continued from page 138

Tree

Festive Gift Bags

Continued from page 138

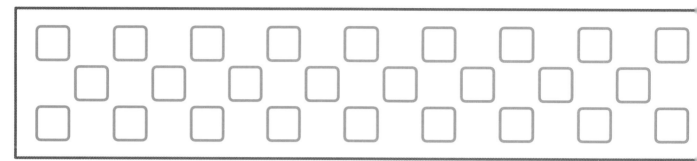

Checkered Pattern

"Let It Snow" Door Hanger

Continued from page 143

Earmuff
Cut 2 from sponge

Snowman Head
Cut 1 from sponge

Snowman Body
Cut 1 from sponge

Banner
Cut 1 from white craft foam

"We Believe In Angels"

Continued from page 136

3-D paint; highlight angel bodies and add dots to i's in lettering with silver 3-D paint. Let dry for 24 hours.

9. Brush entire piece with one or two coats of matte sealer, letting sealer dry for 2 hours between coats, and letting piece dry for 72 hours after final coat.

10. Pull gold cord ends through holes in plaque from back to front; knot on front of plaque. ●

Cookies & Milk Set

Continued from page 144

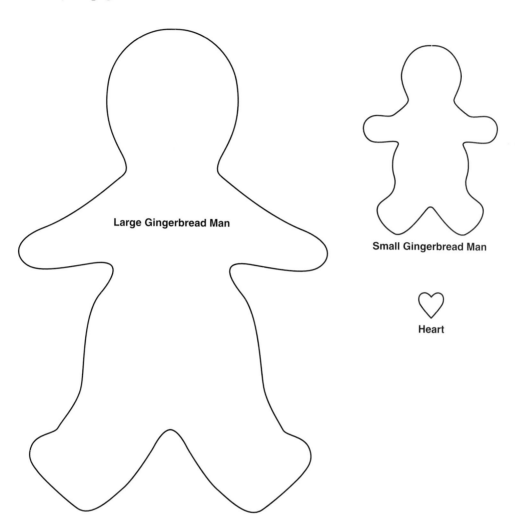

Large Gingerbread Man

Small Gingerbread Man

Heart

Festive Felt Cookies

Continued from page 146

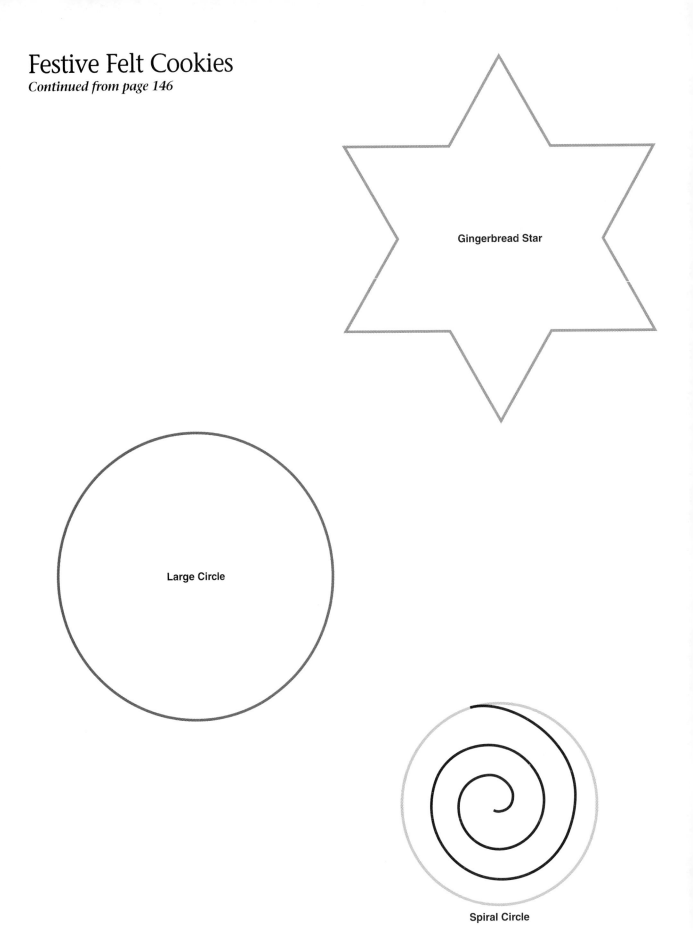

Gingerbread Star

Large Circle

Spiral Circle

Product Guide

When looking for a specific material, first check your local craft and retail stores.
If you are unable to locate a product locally, contact the manufacturers listed below
for the closest retail source in your area, or a mail-order source.

3M
3M Center
Building 304-01-01
St. Paul, MN 55144-1000
(800) 364-3577

Adhesive Technologies Inc.
3 Merrill Industrial Dr.
Hampton, NH 03842-1995
(800) 458-3486
www.adhesivetech.com

Aleene's
Div. of Duncan Enterprises
5673 E. Shields Ave.
Fresno, CA 93727
(800) 237-2642

Amaco/American Art Clay Co. Inc.
4717 W. 16th St.
Indianapolis, IN 46222-2598
(800) 374-1600
www.amaco.com

American Traditional Stencils
442 First New Hampshire Turnpike
Northwood, NH 03261-9754
(800) 278-3624
Fax (800) 448-6654

B&B Products Inc.
P.O. Box 428
Allendale, SC 29810
(888) 382-4255
Fax: (877) 329-3824

**Beacon Adhesives/Signature Mktg.
& Mfg.**
P.O. Box 427
Wyckoff, NJ 07481
(800) 865-7238
Fax (973) 427-2906

The Beadery
P.O. Box 178
Hope Valley, RI 02832
(401) 539-2432

Blumenthal Lansing Co.
1929 Main St.
Lansing, IA 52151
(800) 553-4158

Bucilla Corp.
1 Oak Ridge Rd.
Humboldt Industrial Park
Hazleton, PA 18201-9764
(800) 233-3239

Coats & Clark
Consumer Service
P.O. Box 12229
Greenville, SC 26912-0229
(800) 648-1479
www.coatsandclark.com

Comotion Rubber Stamps Inc.
2711 E. Elvira Rd.
Tucson, AZ 85706
(800) 257-1288
www.comotion.com

CPE Felt
541 Buffalo/W. Springs Hwy.
Union, SC 29379
(800) 327-0059
www.cpe-felt.com

Crafter's Pick by API
520 Cleveland Ave.
Albany, CA 94710
(510) 526-7616
Fax: (510) 524-0573
www.crafterspick.com

The Cranston Collection
469 Seventh Ave.
New York, NY 10018

Creative Beginnings
P.O. Box 1330
Morro Bay, CA 93442
(800) 367-1739

D&CC
428 S. Zelta
Wichita, KS 67207
(800) 835-3013

Daler-Rowney/Robert Simmons Inc.
2 Corporate Dr.
Cranbury, NJ 08512-9584
(800) 278-1783

Darice Inc.
Mail-order source:
Bolek's
P.O. Box 465
330 N. Tuscarawas Ave.
Dover, OH 44622
(330) 364-8878

DecoArt
P.O. Box 386
Stanford, KY 40484
(800) 367-3047

Delta Technical Coatings Inc.
2550 Pellissier Pl.
Whittier, CA 90601-1505
(800) 423-4135

DMC Corp.
Hackensack Avenue, Bldg. 10-A
South Kearny, NJ 07032-4688
(800) 275-4117
www.dmc-usa.com

DMD Industries Inc.
1205 ESI Dr.
Springdale, AR
www.dmdind.com
(501) 750-8929

Duncan Enterprises
5673 E. Shields Ave.
Fresno, CA 93727
(559) 291-4444
www.duncan-enterprises.com

Fairfield
88 Rose Hill Ave.
Danbury, CT 06810
(203) 744-2090

Fiskars
7811 W. Stewart Ave.
Wausau, WI 54401
(800) 950-0203 EXT. 1277
www.fiskars.com

Forster Inc. / Diamond Brands
1800 Cloquet Ave.
Cloquet, MN 55720
(218) 879-6700

Highsmith
W 5527 Hwy. 106
Ft. Atkinson, WI 53538
(800) 554-4661

Koh-I-Noor
100 North St.
Bloomsbury, NJ 08804
(908) 479-8160

Krylon
31500 Solon Rd.
Solon, OH 44139
(216) 498-2331

Kunin Felt Co. / Foss Mfg. Co. Inc.
P.O. Box 5000
Hampton, NH 03842-5000
(800) 292-7900

Lara's Crafts / Div. of Woodworks
4220 Clay Ave.
Fort Worth, TX 76117
(817) 581-9493

Loew-Cornell Inc.
563 Chestnut Ave.
Teaneck, NJ 07666
(201) 836-7070

Magnetic Specialty Inc.
707 Gilman St.
Marietta, OH 45750
(614) 373-1558
www.magspec.com

Mill Hill / Gay Bowles Sales Inc.
P.O. Box 1060
Janesville, WI 53545
(800) 447-1332

Miller Woodcrafts Inc.
10642 Pullman Ct.
Rancho Cucamonga, CA 91730
(800) 990-9609
www.millerwoodcrafts.com

National Artcraft
7996 Darrow Rd.
Twinsburg, OH 44087
(888) 937-2723
www.nationalartcraft.com

**C.M. Offray & Son
Lion Ribbon Co. Inc.**
Route 24, Box 601
Chester, NJ 07930-0601
(800) 551-LION
www.offray.com

One & Only Creations
P.O. Box 2730
Napa, CA 94558
(800) 262-6768

**Pellon / Div. of Freudenberg
Nonwovens**
1040 Avenue of the Americas, 14th floor
New York, NY 10018
(800) 248-5938

Personal Stamp Exchange
360 Sutton Place
Santa Rosa, CA 95407
(707) 588-8058

Plaid Enterprises Inc.
1649 International Ct.
Norcross, GA 30093
(800) 842-4197
www.plaidonline.com

Pres-On Corp.
1020 S. Westgate Dr.
Addison, IL 60101
(800) 323-1745
www.preson.com

Provo Craft
Mail-order source
Creative Express
295 W. Center St.
Provo, UT 84601-4430
(800) 563-8679
www.creativeexpress.com

Royal Golden Taklon
6949 Kennedy Ave.
Hammond, IN 46311
(219) 845-5666

Sakura of America
30780 San Clemente St.
Hayward, CA 94544
(800) 776-6257
express@sakuraofamerica.com

Sculpey III
Polyform Products Co.
1901 Estes
Elk Grove Village, IL 60007
(847) 427-0020

Speedball Art Products
P.O. Box 5157
Statesville, NC 28687
(800) 898-7224

Therm O Web
770 Glenn Ave.
Wheeling, IL 60090
(847) 520-5200

Tolin' Station
P.O. Box 49068
Greensboro, NC 27419

True Colors International
4275 Steve Reynolds Blvd.
Atlanta, GA 30093
(404) 923-6444

Tsukineko Inc.
15411 N. E. 95th St.
Redmond, WA 98052
(800) 769-6633
www.tsukineko.com

Tulip /Div. of Duncan Enterprises
5673 E. Shields Ave,
Fresno, CA 93727
(800) 237-2642

Walnut Hollow
1409 St. Rd. 23
Dodgeville, WI 53533-2112
(800) 950-5101

Wang's
4250 E. Shelby Dr.
Memphis, TN 38118
(901) 362-2111
www.wangs.com

The Warm Company
954 E. Union St.
Seattle, WA 98122
(800) 234-WARM
www.adhost.com/warmcompany/
products.html

**Westrim Crafts/
Western Trimming Corp.**
9667 Canoga Ave.
Chatsworth, CA 91311
(818) 998-8550

Wichelt Imports Inc.
N162 Hwy. 35
Stoddard, WI 54658
(608) 788-4600
Fax (608) 788-6040
www.wichelt.com

Wimpole Street Creations
Mail-order source:
Barrett House
P.O. Box 540585
North Salt Lake, UT 84054-0585
(801) 299-0700

Woodworks
4521 Anderson Blvd.
Forth Worth, TX 76117
(817) 581-5230

Wrights
P.O. Box 398
West Warren, MA 01092
(413) 436-7732, ext. 445

General Instructions

Materials List

In addition to the materials listed for each craft, some of the following crafting supplies may be needed to complete your projects. No doubt most of these are already on hand in your "treasure chest" of crafting aids. If not, you may want to gather them now so that you'll be able to complete each design quickly and without a hitch!

General Crafts

- Scissors
- Pencil
- Ruler
- Tracing paper
- Craft knife
- Heavy-duty craft cutters or wire nippers

Painted Items

- Paper towels
- Paper or plastic foam plate or tray to use as a disposable paint palette for holding and mixing paints
- Plastic—a garbage bag, grocery sack etc.—to protect your work surface
- Container of water for rinsing and cleaning brushes

Fabric Projects

- Iron and ironing board
- Pressing cloth
- Basic sewing notions
- Rotary cutter and self-healing mat
- Air-soluble markers
- Tailor's chalk

Needlework Designs

- Embroidery scissors
- Iron and ironing board
- Thick terry towel
- Air-soluble markers
- Tailor's chalk

Reproducing Patterns & Templates

The patterns provided in this book are shown right side up, as they should look on the finished project; a few oversize patterns that need to be enlarged are clearly marked. Photocopiers with enlarging capabilities are readily available at copy stores and office supply stores. Simply copy the page, setting the photocopier to enlarge the pattern to the percentage indicated.

Patterns that do not need to be enlarged may be reproduced simply by placing a piece of

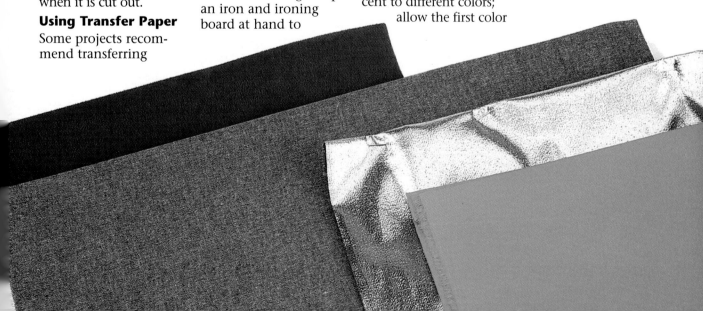

tracing paper or vellum over the pattern in the book, and tracing the outlines carefully with a pencil or other marker.

Once you've copied your pattern pieces, cut them out and use these pieces as templates to trace around. Secure them as needed with pins or pattern weights.

If you plan to reuse the patterns or if the patterns are more intricate, with sharp points, etc., make sturdier templates by gluing the copied page of patterns onto heavy cardboard or template plastic. Let the glue dry, then cut out the pieces using a craft knife.

Depending on the application, it may be preferable to trace the patterns onto the *wrong* side of the fabric or other material so that no tracing lines will be visible from the front; in this case, make sure you place the *right* side of the pattern piece against the *wrong* side of the fabric, paper or other material so that the piece will face the right direction when it is cut out.

Using Transfer Paper

Some projects recommend transferring patterns to wood or another material with transfer paper. Read the manufacturer's instructions before beginning.

Lay tracing paper over the printed pattern and trace it carefully. Then place transfer paper, transfer side down, on wood or other material to be marked. Lay traced pattern on top. Secure layers with low-tack masking tape or tacks to keep pattern and transfer paper from shifting while you work.

Using a stylus, pen or other marking implement, retrace the pattern lines using smooth, even pressure to transfer design onto surface.

Working With Fabrics

Read instructions carefully; take seam allowances into consideration when cutting fabrics.

If colorfastness is a concern, launder fabrics first without using fabric softener. Press with an iron before using. Keep an iron and ironing board at hand to press seams and pattern pieces as you work.

Pattern markings may be transferred to fabrics with air-soluble markers or tailor's chalk. For permanent markings on fabric, use the specific pens and paints listed with each project. It is a good idea to always test the pen or marker on a scrap of fabric to check for bleeding, etc.

Painted Designs

Disposable paper or plastic foam plates, including supermarket meat trays, make good palettes for pouring and mixing paints.

The success of a painted project often depends a great deal on the care taken in the initial preparations, including sanding, applying primer, and/or applying a base coat of color. Follow instructions carefully in this regard.

Take special care when painting sections adjacent to different colors; allow the first color to dry so that the second will not run or mix. When adding designs atop a painted base, let the base coat dry thoroughly first.

If you will be mixing media, such as drawing with marking pens on a painted surface, test the process and your materials on scraps to make sure there will be no unsightly running or bleeding.

Keep your work surface and your tools clean. Clean brushes promptly in the manner recommended by the paint manufacturer; many acrylics can be cleaned up with soap and water, while other paints may require a solvent of some kind. Suspend your paintbrushes by their handles to dry so that the cleaning fluid drains out completely without bending the bristles.

Project/Technique Index

Crafter's Notes

Crafter's Notes